C000067951

NORFOLK VILLAINS

ROGUES, RASCALS **AND** REPROBATES

NORFOLK VILLAINS

ROGUES, RASCALS AND REPROBATES

NEIL R. STOREY

The History Press

First published 2012

The History Press
The Mill, Brimscombe Port
Stroud, Gloucestershire, GL5 2QG
www.thehistorypress.co.uk

© Neil R. Storey, 2012

The right of Neil R. Storey to be identified as the Author
of this work has been asserted in accordance with the
Copyrights, Designs and Patents Act 1988.

All rights reserved. No part of this book may be reprinted
or reproduced or utilised in any form or by any electronic,
mechanical or other means, now known or hereafter invented,
including photocopying and recording, or in any information
storage or retrieval system, without the permission in writing
from the Publishers.

British Library Cataloguing in Publication Data.
A catalogue record for this book is available from the British Library.

ISBN 978 0 7524 6001 7

Typesetting and origination by The History Press
Printed and bound in Great Britain by
Marston Book Services Limited, Didcot

Contents

Acknowledgements

I have been granted privileged access to numerous public and private archives and collections in preparation for this book, and it is to all those who have opened their doors and collections to me who I wish to extend a personal and very genuine thank you. Once again, whilst researching some of the darkest tales from Norfolk's past, I have met, as well as renewed the acquaintance of, some of the nicest people. I would like to express particular gratitude to my students and audiences for their thoughts and comments. Thanks also to the following, without whose help, kindness, enthusiasm, generosity and knowledge, this book would not have been so enriched: my friend and esteemed fellow crime historian Stewart P. Evans and his good lady Rosie; James Nice; BBC Radio Norfolk; Andrew Selwyn-Crome; Sally Kent; Jean Hunt; Nigel Gant; Dr Vic Morgan; Helen Tovey at *Family Tree* magazine; Norfolk Family History Society; The Tolhouse Museum, Great Yarmouth; The Shirehall Museum and Bridewell at Walsingham; Wymondham Bridewell Museum; Dr Tim Pestell and Marilyn Taylor at Norwich Castle Museum; The Galleries of Justice, Nottingham; Dr John Alban and all the helpful staff at the Norfolk Record Office; University of East Anglia Library; the encyclopaedic knowledge of Michael Bean and Clive Wilkins-Jones, and the superb staff at the Norfolk Heritage Library, Norwich;

King's Lynn Library; Thetford Library (Thetford Norfolk Studies Collection); and to my friends amongst the past and present serving officers of Norfolk Constabulary, especially Peter Pilgram and the late John Mason at the Norfolk Constabulary Archive.

Finally, and by no means least, I thank my family, especially my dear son Lawrence and my beloved Molly, for their love, interest and support in the research of this book.

The Cranworth stocks; a rural curiosity when this photograph was taken in the early twentieth century, but once a robust, very real punishment and a legal requirement for every parish in England.

Introduction

Norfolk is a truly remarkable county of beauty; mellow land-
scapes and seascapes inhabited, in the main, by good honest
country folk, but the following pages provide a dark mirror
to its past, revealed through a plethora of crimes and the stories of those who committed them. There are a few notorious
tales from the distant past and a handful of those you may have
heard of before – stories of characters so infamous, devious and
dreadful that they must be included in a volume such as this.
However, the majority of tales contained in this book have
remained untold for over a century and are drawn from the
assize records, witness statements, newspapers and broadsides
contemporary to each case.

The stories herein date predominantly from the nineteenth
century and thus contain many accounts from the early years of
the new police forces established in the county at that time. In the
early nineteenth century there was no police force; law and order
was maintained in the county by magistrates, those appointed
as city and parish constables – with occasional assistance from
Special Constables recruited under emergency powers when
required – and even the military during instances of rioting when
times were hard, livelihoods were threatened or food became pro-
hibitively expensive.

Modern policing in Norfolk and for much of the country began in 1835, when the Municipal Corporations Act of 1835 was passed. Among other matters, the Act required every borough in England and Wales to establish a Watch Committee, who had the duty of appointing constables 'for the preserving of the peace'. The jurisdiction of the borough constables extended to any place within seven miles of the borough. The County Police Act followed in 1839, which enabled Justices of the Peace to establish police forces in their counties, but this was not compulsory and constabularies were only established in twenty-five out of fifty-five counties. Norfolk took the opportunity to form one of the first county constabularies, but it was only with the passing of the County and Borough Police Act (1856) that their provision became mandatory.

Parish lock-ups and stocks were still being maintained and used into the middle years of the nineteenth century. Although it may appear to be a draconian measure, the use of lock-ups is reasonable when you consider that, when in use, police transport usually meant one horse and trap per area. Lock-ups provided a secure place to hold any arrested felon until transport arrived, and were especially useful if the felon was a drunk and/or violent individual and needed to sober up or cool down before they were brought before the magistrates.

The stocks, however, were medieval; in fact they were the oldest and most widely used punitive device and were still in use for the punishment of minor offenders during the nineteenth century. For the country magistrate and the prison system as a whole the use of parish stocks saved time and money. A person brought before the Bench found guilty of minor offences, such as drunk and disorderly behaviour, would serve their sentence without the involvement of prison admission, paperwork, government-issue clothing and food. The punishment would involve the miscreant being locked in the stocks for a few hours in the space of a day. By the 1850s, the use of the stocks was petering out and the last recorded use of the stock in England was at Rugby in 1865.

By the 1840s, Norfolk had five separate police forces; there were borough forces at Thetford, Great Yarmouth, King's Lynn and Norwich, with the rest of the county served by Norfolk

Rural Police. Each of these forces were governed by their own watch committees, which would have their own by-laws to maintain and their own Chief Constable. In 1854, Francis White's *Directory of Norfolk* reflects those early years by stating:

> County Police: Headquarters (for the present) at Hingham, but they will be removed to the Castle Hill, Norwich on completion of the new station house, which it is expected will be about the end of the year 1854. The Force consists of 1 Chief Constable; 1 Deputy Chief Constable; 14 Superintendents; 7 Inspectors; 3 Sergeants and 155 Police Constables [...] The erection of the New Station Houses at Norwich, Acle, Dereham, Docking, Harling (East) and Pulham St Mary Magdalen is to be proceeded with immediately, but those at Caistor-next-Yarmouth, Cromer, Diss, Litcham, Mundford, Reepham, Smallburgh, Walsingham, Walsoken and Watton at a later period.

With the exception of Thetford Police, which joined with the county police during the nineteenth century, this structure of borough and county police forces remained in place into the latter half of the twentieth century. Today, Norfolk Constabulary employs over 8,000 staff to help maintain law and order in the county.

Chief Constable George Black (seated centre and holding the umbrella) with the Senior Officers of Norfolk Constabulary in 1880. (Norfolk Constabulary Archive)

NORFOLK, } TO WIT {

A CALENDAR

Of the Prisoners now in the Custody of the Sheriff of the said County, for Trial at the Lent Assizes, to be holden at Thetford, in the said County, on Saturday, the 15th day of March, 1828, before the Right Honourable Charles, Lord Tenterden, Chief Justice of our Lord the King, assigned to hold pleas before the King himself, and the Honourable Sir William Garrow, Knight, one of the Barons of our said Lord the King, of his Court of Exchequer, Justices of our said Lord the King, assigned to deliver the aforesaid Gaol of the Prisoners therein being.

FELONS FOR TRIAL.

1 THOMAS BALLS aged 2 26, and DAVID TUNMORE, aged 19,   Committed August 20, 1827, by R. Plumptre, J. Harvey, J. S. Patteson, and Wm. Blake, Esqrs. charged on the oath of Jared Horner, of Scottow, farmer, and others, with having, on the night of the 14th of this month, or early the following morning, burglariously broken into his dwelling-house, and stolen thereout various articles of provision and linen.

3 WILLIAM SPINKS, aged 19,   Committed Oct. 1, 1827, by Rev. George Waddington, Clk. charged on the oath of Ann Foyster, and others, with having, in the night of the 29th of Sept. last, burglariously entered her dwelling-house, and stolen therefrom a purse, containing a bank note for one pound and three sovereigns.

4 JOHN HOWARD, aged 5 23, BENJAMIN WRIGHT, aged 27, and 6 JOHN QUADLING, aged 20,   Committed Oct. 13, 1827, by H. N. Burroughes, Esq. and Rev. J. D. Borton, Clk. charged on the oath of John Jay, of Buckenham, alehouse-keeper, and others, with having, in the night of the 3d of this month, or early the following morning, burglariously broken and entered his dwelling-house, and stolen thereout two gallons of rum, two gallons of gin, two stone bottles, and about four stone of pork ; and from out of an out-house, which was broken open, thirteen cheeses.

7 HENRY BOON, aged 20, 8 GEORGE BRAMMAR, aged 21, and JANE 9 LEWIS, alias BRAMMAR, aged 20,   Committed Nov. 3, 1827, by Rev. Edw. Marsham and Rev. Robt. Norris, Clks. charged on the oath of John Sharpin, of Tattersett, with having, on the 15th of Oct. last, between the hours of eight and nine o'clock in the evening, robbed him, on the King's highway, of a silver watch and a quantity of silver.

10 JOHN MORTIMER ALGAR, aged 29, and 11 JOHN PALMER, aged 21,   Committed November 12, 1827, by Rev. Chancellor Yonge, Clk. charged on the oath of Edward Amond Johnson, and others with having uttered, on the 20th of October last, at Cranwich, a counterfeit Bank of England Bank of England note for £5 ; also with having uttered, at Great Cressingham, on the 30th of the same month, another counterfeit Bank of England note for £5 ; and another counterfeit Bank of England note, of the same amount, on the 1st of November, at Foulden.
The said John Mortimer Algar is also further charged, before the same Magistrate, on the oath of the said Edward Amond Johnson, and others, with having, on the 23d of October last, uttered a counterfeit Bank of England note for £5, at Foulden.

12 WILLIAM HOVELL, aged 28, 13 JOHN BILNEY, aged 42, 14 CHARLES WARD, aged 22,   Committed November 13, 1827, By J. T. Dering, Esq. and Rev. Wm. Hardwicke, Clk. charged on the oath of John Pike, of Wimbotsham, shopkeeper, and others, with having, on the night of the 9th of this month, broken into his shop, and stolen there-out various articles.

15 JOHN ASHLEY, aged 22,   Committed November 20, 1827, by Sir Jacob Astley, Bart. and A. Rawlinson, Esq. charged on the oath of Thomas Leeder, of Barney, blacksmith, and others, with having, on the 14th of this month, stolen from his person a red morocco pocket book, with ten pounds, and sundry papers.

16 JOHN KENNEY, aged 22,   Committed December 19, 1827, by F. T. Quarles, Gent. Coroner for the liberty of the Duchy of Lancaster, charged on the Coroner's inquest with the wilful murder of William Moore, at Brisley.

17 GEORGE BELL, aged 18 16, and SKEET, alias EDMUND WATSON, aged 17,   Committed December 31, 1827, by Sir E. K. Lacon, Bart. Rev. Richard Turner, Clk. Wm. Steward, Esq. and Rev. James Symonds, Clk. charged on the oath of Mary, the wife of John Larke, of Runham, with having, on the 24th of this month, on the King's highway, in Caistor, stolen from a cart, which she was then driving, a bottle of beer, a basket containing grocery goods, and various other articles.

19 JAMES SADD, aged 23, 20 and JOHN RUSSELL, aged 24,   Committed January 1, 1828, by the Rev. Wm. Manning, Clk. charged on the oath of James Smith, of Frenze, gentleman, with having stolen a sheep from him on the 20th December, 1825.

21 JOSEPH PALMER, aged 16,   Committed January 9, 1828, by J. Straccy, John Harvey, and Kerrison Harvey, Esqrs. charged on the oath of James Amis, of Barton Turf, waterman, and others, with having, on the 5th of this month, stolen privately from his person £20 in provincial bank notes.

22 JOSEPH LEE, aged 62,   Committed January 25, 1828, by John Patteson, Esq. charged on the oath of William Smith, of Swardeston, farmer, and others, with having, on the night of the 22d of this month, burglariously broken and entered his dwelling-house, and stolen thereout various articles of provision and cooking utensils.

23 TIMOTHY POTTON, aged 37,   Committed February 4, 1828, by Rev. B. Barker, Clk. charged on the oath of Robert Bussey and others, with having, on the night of the 2d of this month, stolen a sheep from William Colman, of Rockland St. Peter, yeoman.

24 EDWARD EVERETT, aged 21,   Committed February 4, 1828, by E. R. Pratt, J. T. Dering, and G. R. Eyres, Esqrs. charged on the oath of Thomas Joyce, of West Dereham, labourer, with having, on the 1st of this month, stolen from his pocket a canvas purse, containing six half-crowns, five shillings, and five sixpences.

25 MARY CHESNUTT, aged 21,   Committed Feb. 22, 1828, by Rev. Wm. Grigson, Clk. charged on the oath of Smith Wright, of Watton, and others, with having, in the evening of the 13th of the same month, feloniously set fire to and burnt an oat stack, at Merton.

26 RICHARD RICHARDSON, aged 25,   Committed February 22, 1828, by John Freeman, Esq. Mayor of the Borough of Castle Rising, charged on the oath of John Carter, of Roydon, farmer, with having, on the 12th of this month, assaulted him on the King's highway, at South Wootton, within the said borough, and stole his hat.

27 JOHN SPINK, aged 21,   Committed February 26, 1828, by the Right Hon. the Earl of Orford and James Gay, Esq. charged on the oath of William Purdy, of Aylsham, labourer, with having, on the 18th of this month, feloniously stabbed him.

28 JAMES COX, aged 32,   Committed February 26, 1828, by J. Postle and A. Beevor, Esqrs. and Rev. Geo. Preston, Clk. charged on the oath of John Wade, of Weeting, with having, in the night of Friday, the 22d of this month, or early the following morning, stolen a mare from out of a stable in his occupation.

29 JOHN WILLIAMS, aged 45,   Committed August 24, 1827, by Hon. and Rev. Wm. Wodehouse, and received into custody on the 29th of February, 1828, charged on the oath of John Bayfield Nettleship, of Totington, with having, in the night of the 23d, or early in the morning of the 24th of August last, stolen five lambs out of a flock.

30 THOMAS LOVE, aged 43,   Committed March 5, 1828, by Rev. Ellis Burroughes, Clk. charged on the oath of John Pearson, of Tibenham, farmer, with having, in the night of the 3d of this month, or early the following morning, stolen from out of his farm-yard one wether hogget sheep.

31 JONAS CABLE, aged 26,   Committed March 6, 1828, by J. Wright, Esq. charged on the oath of Eli Ruddock, assistant overseer of the poor of North Lopham, with having entered a shed for keeping firing for the poor, with intent to steal the same.

32 WILLIAM DYBALL, aged 51, and ISAAC 33 DYBALL, aged 23,   Committed March 8, 1828, by R. Plumptre and Wm. Blake, Esqrs. and Rev. J. Humfrey, Clk. charged on the oath of Wm. Postle, of Buxton, farmer, and others, with having, on the 29th of February last, or early the following morning, stolen from out of a shed eleven hens.

34 GEORGE MUTEHAM, aged 21,   Committed March 11, 1828, by Rev. Wm. Grigson, charged on the oath of Thomas Jary, of Stow Bedon, farmer, with having stolen a pig, from out of a stye.

35 ELIZABETH LEE, aged 25,   Committed March 12, 1828, by J. Gay, Esq. charged on the oath of William Ward, of the city of Norwich, with having stolen from his person, in the parish of Aylsham, a quantity of silver coin, to the amount of about 45 shillings.

36 WILLIAM SAYER, aged 37 16, and WM. RAYNER,   Committed March 12, 1828, by D. Gurney, Esq. charged on the oath of Stephen Smith and another, with having, on the 23d day of February last, broken into his dwelling-house, at Middleton, and stolen thereout

The Calendar of Prisoners recording the felons and the array of offences they had been charged with; brought before the Norfolk Lent Assizes held at Thetford on 15 March 1828.

Petty Sessions for the Magistrates' Courts were held across the county in public houses and inns. Purpose-built courthouses for Petty Sessions were, for the most part, a nineteenth-century development. The local Bench would be occupied by magistrates, otherwise known as Justices of the Peace. Many of them would have been upstanding members of the local community, usually land owners too – so woe betide if you were a poacher! Petty Sessions each had allotted geographical areas across the county, known as Divisions, that would sit at appointed times, two to four times per month. In 1890, the Norfolk Petty Session Divisions were recorded as Acle, Aylsham, East Dereham, Docking, Downham, Harling, Holt, Loddon, North Walsham, Norwich, Pulham, Swaffham, Terrington, Little Walsingham and Wymondham.

More serious cases, such as petty larceny and assault, would be tried at the General Quarter Sessions, which were held four times a year at the Shirehall, Norwich, for the eastern division of the county; Swaffham Shirehall for the western division; Norwich Guildhall for the city, and the Town Halls of Great Yarmouth and King's Lynn for offences committed in those boroughs.

The most serious crimes would be referred to the assizes; indeed, all crimes that could receive a capital sentence would

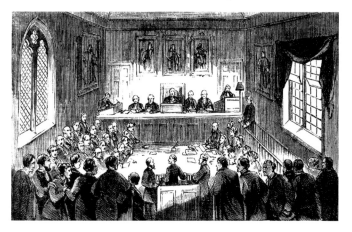

Examination of the accused at the Norwich Assizes, in the courtroom at the Guildhall in 1869.

ultimately be brought before the Courts of Assize – presided over by the judges of the King's Bench Division of the High Court of Justice. These judges served in the seven circuits of England and Wales on commissions of 'oyer and terminer', setting up court and summoning juries at the established 'Assize Towns'. Under a system that dated back to Henry II, assizes for the county of Norfolk were held at Thetford at Lent and the Summer Assizes were held Norwich. This led to the time-consuming, uncomfortable and risky transport of prisoners from Norwich Castle Gaol to Thetford for trial. After numerous petitions, the Norfolk Lent Assizes were formally moved to Norwich under the Norwich Assize Bill in 1832, and the old Thetford gaol was

The Downfall of Poor Dicky

OR THE TROWSE INFORMER

BY CHARLES BLACK

Now you good folks of——a story I'll tell,
Its concerning an informer in Trowse he do dwell
Why he is a tall fellow if the truth I must tell,
They say this informer he do come from H-ll.

Now if a poor fellow work on the railroad
Why beware of this informer he will do you no good
He will poke in his nose and do all that he can
No doubt tis on purpose to hurt a poor man.

Why this informer is known if the truth I must tell known very well,
He have been a rogue from his cradle thats
Why Dicky I tell you, you are of no use
So its no use your trying to get on the police.

Now you Publicans all mind what you are about
By chance this informer may poke in his snout
Why he is sure to trepan you with a snare and a grin you in.
And its a chance of ten thousand but he will let

Oh what will become of poor Dicky by & by
Why there's no one will employ him I will tell you for why

mouse
Why he is forc'd to keep in holes lay still as a
No doubt in a short time he's in a workhouse

And if a piece of iron the workmen lay by
This informer they say walk about as a spy
Why he go to the police and give information
In hopes there's no doubt to gain a situation

Why its no use dear Dicky you a situation wont get
You will never be a policeman you need not fret
For the colonal wont have you nor no such a man you can
So you may pack up your dud's and do the best

Why a poor man with a family in Lakenham dwell
Who is deprived of his living the truth I must tell
He is deprived of a living through this informing man
Why he is going to h-ll as fast as he can

So now to conclude and to make an end
I hope this poor man will soon find a friend
While Dicky the informer be as thin as a mouse
And be forced to pull Okeham in a workhouse,

Printed for Charles Black.

An unusual nineteenth-century broadside which relates, in rhyme and with little genuine sympathy, the downfall of 'Poor Dicky', the Trowse informer.

converted into a police station. From 1832, the Norfolk Circuit of Assizes rotated around the counties of Buckinghamshire, Bedfordshire, Huntingdonshire, Cambridgeshire, Norfolk and Suffolk, together with the City of Norwich and the jurisdictions of Ely, King's Lynn and Great Yarmouth.

Justice was not always swift for those who stood accused of the most serious offences. The Norfolk Assizes were only held twice a year. If a suspect was brought into custody for a serious crime shortly after the last assizes, he or she would face the judicial process of appearing before the local magistrates or Coroner's Court then a long wait before their trial at the next county assizes.

Within this volume are stories of criminals who tempted fate and were caught and suffered the full rigour of the law, while other cases expose the shortcomings of the legal system of the past, when there was little or no forensic knowledge and before fingerprints were recognised as key to identifying criminals; a time when the motive and many clues may point to a suspect, but at the trial the evidence was insufficient to secure a conviction. Many of the cases also have surprising touchstones that can be found in our modern world, and perhaps, in some instances, lead us to consider how much has changed in human nature or crime in general over the last century or so. I leave it to you the reader to decide if the sentences were just and fitting for the crimes described herein.

Neil R. Storey
Norfolk, 2012

Chapter One

Highway Robbery

The Dandy Highwayman

Joseph Beeton was a handsome young man who had just turned twenty years old when he was brought before the Recorder at the Quarter Sessions at King's Lynn on Monday, 20 January 1783, charged with robbing the north mail coach on 19 November 1782. The evidence presented at the trial revealed that Beeton had concealed himself in a clump of thorn bushes beside the Saddlebow Road, beyond the Long Bridge that crossed the River Nar. When the elderly 'post boy', who had left King's Lynn to connect with the Wisbech coach, drove by in his cart, Beeton climbed into the branches of a nearby tree, dropped onto the coach, and made off with the mail bags, worth in excess of £1,000. A handsome reward was offered for the highway robber and Beeton was given up. Arrested and held in Lynn Gaol, Beeton did not resign himself to his fate and managed to escape, fleeing to an inn at Castle Acre. The landlord, however, grew suspicious of the young rascal and communicated his suspicions to the authorities at Lynn; Beeton was recaptured and escorted back, in irons, by an armed guard.

Richard Beeton the dandy highwayman, depicted in irons awaiting his fate in the condemned cell in Lynn Gaol, 1783.

Beeton, being young and attractive, drew considerable public sympathy, as did his story, for he claimed he had been drawn to commit the crime by a supposed friend. Many gentlemen of Lynn were moved by the plight of poor Joseph Beeton, so much so that a subscription was entered into and money collected in order to employ counsel to plead for him at his trial. Even with a fine advocate, after a trial of six hours, Beeton was found guilty and received sentence of death. About eleven o'clock on the morning of Monday, 17 February 1783, Beeton was conveyed from Lynn Gaol in a mourning coach to the gallows near Southgates (not far from the spot where the robbery was committed), attended by two clergymen, the Revd Mr Horsfall and the Revd Mr Merrest. One account of the event would remark: 'The spirit of the prisoner, the constancy of his friends, and the church-parade made bright episodes in a dreadful scene.'

Beeton's behaviour, both before and at the place of execution, was recorded as truly devout and exemplary, but then 'uncommon pains had been taken by the Revd Mr Horsfall to prepare him for his awful fate.' After praying some time with great fervency and a hymn being sung by the singers from St Margaret's Church, the rope was fixed around his neck. Not long had this been done before Beeton threw himself off the platform and died amid the pitying tears of the spectators, whose numbers were upwards of 5,000. Beeton's body was covered in pitch and gibbeted near the scene as a warning to others for years after, and even when the gibbet was no more, his name lingered on – the clump of trees near the site became known as 'Beeton's Bush'.

'Mad Tom' the Highwayman

Jeremiah Pratt, alias John Wilson, known to most as 'Mad Tom', was tried and found guilty of three indictments for horse stealing and was sentenced to death at the Norfolk Lent Assizes, held at Thetford in 1746. After his condemnation, Pratt confessed to robbing the Yarmouth stagecoach on three occasions; the Norwich stagecoach once, near the windmill at St Stephen's Gates; and to robbing Mr Long of Spixworth, just outside of Magdalen Gates. Indeed, he claimed he had 'stolen more horses than the infamous Turpin.' In the hope that no other should be punished for the crimes he had committed, Pratt requested that those persons who had had any horses stolen should apply to him at the County Gaol and there they would receive information of not only the robbery, but also where the horses were disposed of, if he had been involved. Returned to Norwich for execution, he met his end in front of a large and rowdy crowd upon Castle Hill on 12 April 1746.

The exterior of St Stephen's Gates, Norwich, during the eighteenth century.

Three Gentlemen of the Road

In reality there were few dandy highwaymen, but there is evidence to suggest that some women were drawn to criminal types or 'bad boys', especially if they were young and handsome. Indeed, even the sympathies of crowds could sometimes be swayed in favour of these youthful criminals, such as Michael Moore, William Fletcher and William Skipper.

August 1780, Benjamin Bell, John Fuller and Turner Thurrold had been drinking at The Swan in Swaffham and were about to head back to their homes in Castle Acre, on horseback, when they were joined by two strangers, also on horseback, who said they were going on the same road, so they all set out together. When they had travelled less than a mile from Swaffham the two strangers launched an attack upon their travelling companions, demanding their money. Mr Bell jumped off his horse and got into an adjoining close, while Fuller and Thurrold galloped on; all three escaped being robbed.

The highwaymen pursued Fuller and Thurrold but met John Rice, a Swaffham glazier, and waylaid him instead, robbing him of his silver watch, four shillings and six pence. While in the act of robbing Mr Rice, Mr Galloway, a farrier from Castle Acre, passed them. Once they had finished robbing Rice, the highwaymen set off in pursuit of Galloway. Knocking him off his horse, the highwaymen beat him cruelly then robbed him of his shoes and one pound three shillings in money. They then returned towards Swaffham, passing Mr Rice. They were about 200 yards from the town when they encountered Mr Jermyn, a considerable farmer of Weasenham. The highwaymen beat him, tore his breeches and robbed him of his hat, boots, spurs, silver watch, around thirty-five pounds in cash and a banker's bill for five guineas.

One of the highwaymen's horses managed to break free while they were robbing Mr Jermyn; unfortunately for Mr Rice, who was travelling back up the road, the highwaymen dismounted him and took his horse, riding into Swaffham in pursuit of their lost horse. By this point, Mr Jermyn had managed to return to the town and raise the alarm. Several people instantly mounted their horses and set off after the highwaymen. Thomas Marcon of Swaffham overtook one of them at the end of town, but as he lifted his stick to knock the robber off his horse, the highwayman threw himself off and escaped into the fields. The fugitive was, however, discovered in a ditch and was properly secured, along with the two horses. The other highwayman got off Mr Rice's horse and, owing to the darkness of the night, averted capture. However, Mr Bowker of Swaffham, in company with Mr Thurrold and Mr Galloway, made a fresh pursuit the following morning and overtook the highwayman in the middle of the town of Wisbech, where they managed to pull him off his horse and secure him.

Investigations revealed that the first highwayman was one Michael Moore, a butcher of Bourne in Lincolnshire. When taken he was found to have Mr Jermyn's hat on his head, Mr Rice's watch and Mr Galloway's money and pocketbook in his pocket. The other man had Mr Jermyn's watch and two other silver watches in his pocket, with about £30 in cash and a purse, with gold gauge and key, which belonged to Mr Jermyn. This highwayman gave his name as William Smith (real name William Fletcher), a chimney sweep by trade and likewise a Lincolnshire man. They were both committed to Norwich Castle by James Nelthorpe, Esq.

The latter highwayman gang was soon identified as one that had been responsible for numerous depravations upon the roads of West Norfolk and eastern England. The horses they had been riding were also stolen and were subsequently recognised by two gentlemen – one from Leicestershire, the other from Stamford, in Lincolnshire. One of the watches taken from Smith was also identified as belonging to a Leicestershire tradesman, who had been robbed by the gang some time past; they also relieved him of nearly thirty pounds. The inhabitants of Swaffham were praised for their 'uncommon spirit and alacrity in pursuing and taking two such dangerous fellows.'

On 15 March 1781, before Alexander Lord Loughborough at the Norfolk Assizes, William Fletcher (alias Smith), aged nineteen, and Michael Moore, aged seventeen, were joined by two other highwaymen from their gang, namely William Skipper (alias John Love), aged twenty-three, and John Ewston (alias

Hewston). They were all found guilty of highway robbery and sentenced to death. Ewston was fortunate and received His Majesty's pardon, on the condition that he entered into the service of the East India Company. Fletcher, Moore and Skipper were left to hang. Penitent and behaving in a manner becoming of their situation upon the Castle Hill gallows on 7 April 1781, the *Norwich Mercury* reported:

> [...] the fatal three acknowledged justly to suffer and asked forgiveness of all whom they had injured. Skipper exhorted all youth to take a proper warning of their untimely end and after a few moments in most fervent prayer they were launched into eternity amidst the sympathetic tears of thousands of spectators.

A postscript may be found in the *Norfolk Chronicle* of 5 January 1782, which reported John Ewston set out, well guarded, for London, in order to be put on board an Indiaman.

The Old Game

Cook March was born at Hainford to poor but honest parents. His father was a hog-gelder and the young March followed in his father's trade for some years, but did not like to be 'under any restraint' and left home. When he was twenty-four, he fell in with Elizabeth Garwood, described as 'a most abandoned woman.' March claimed that Garwood attempted to get him to poison her husband – she even gave the powder to him, but he washed it away down the gutter. March tried to escape from Garwood's clutches by moving to Bungay but she followed him, and said that if he did not take her back she would drown herself. She walked away and, fearing she may carry out her threat, March persuaded her to come back and they remained together.

It then seems that they started working the prostitute scam, whereby Garwood would entice a man then March would suddenly appear and assault the mark, claiming to be furious that he had caught the man with his 'wife'. After giving the mark a good beating, he would then relieve them of any valuables.

Such acts were not normally committed on main roads but in the darker, quieter lanes where prostitutes would take their clients; however, the crime was still classified as highway robbery. March was convicted at the Norwich City Assizes on 11 August 1794, for violent assault upon Mr Eaton, who he had 'caught' with Garwood on Ber Street Gates in Eaton Hall Lane. In his confession, March admitted to violently assaulting Eaton, claiming:

> [...] we both fell in the struggle, I got up and said I will make you pay dearly for being with my wife, we fell together a second time, when Mr Eaton said, 'For God's sake spare my life' he then gave me 6s 6d. I then let him go. I gave Sally Fox 6d to hold her tongue and gave 1s also to Garwood.

Marsh went on to confess to robbing a Mr Howlett, who he had beaten and robbed of a guinea and a £20 note under similar circumstances. March met his end at the City Gallows on 6 September 1794.

A Female Highway Robber

On 27 February 1823, Farmer Disney's sixteen-year-old daughter was on a shopping trip in Yarmouth – accompanied by a male and female servant – when she encountered a young woman named Mary Durrant (aged twenty-three), who she had known from her home parish of Reedham for a number of years. Durrant had clearly fallen on hard times since she had left. As they set out to return home at the end of the day, Durrant accompanied them as far as Fritton before she bade them goodnight and left.

As Miss Disney and the two servants made their way along the Haddiscoe Dam on that darkening February evening, a figure she initially thought was a man in female attire approached her and demanded her money, threatening to cut her throat if she did not instantly comply. As she issued the demand the highway robber put her hand in her bosom as if to take out a knife. Although a scarf was drawn up across the lower part of her face, Miss Disney could see enough to discern the clothing, build and other features as those of Durrant. On hearing the dreadful threat, the servants fled and Miss Disney was left to face the robber alone. Terrified by the confrontation she handed over a Morocco purse containing twenty-eight shillings and a bundle of goods, including expensive luxuries such as oranges and lace. The robber then made her escape and left Miss Disney to walk home alone. The servants who had fled had, at least, raised the alarm in Haddiscoe and a number of local people were on their way to assist her. Mr Hatch, the coachman of the Yarmouth Star coach, drove up shortly after and was also given information about the robbery. On arrival at St Olave's Bridge, he was hailed by the landlord of the public house there and asked if he had room to take a young woman to Yarmouth; he replied that he had, and the minute the woman made her appearance the coachman realised this was the woman described to him at Haddiscoe. He placed her inside and asked one of his friends to get in and keep an eye on her, but not to let his suspicions be known.

On the arrival of the coach at Yarmouth, Pratt, the Mayor's Officer, was sent for, who took her to his own house. He examined the bundle she had with her and found the distinctive

The Great Yarmouth Tolhouse Gaol, 1819.

contents stolen from Miss Disney and, on a further search, discovered the purse with its contents behind her stays. Subsequent
investigations also revealed that Durrant had obtained three
pairs of stays and three caps under false pretences, from Bessey
and Underwood, milliners in Broad Row, Great Yarmouth;
items that she had afterwards pawned in the town.

Durrant was held at the Great Yarmouth Tolhouse until she
was brought up before the magistrates for the county, assembled at the Feathers Inn in Yarmouth Market Place. After a short
hearing, Durrant was committed to Norwich Castle to await
trial and appeared before the Norfolk Assizes at Thetford, on
Saturday 15 March 1823. She pleaded guilty and a sentence
of death was passed upon her, but she was assured of mercy
on account of her youth and her sentence was commuted to
imprisonment.

Escape from Bigod's Tower

After a long day on his rounds James Rayner, a baker of
Middleton, near King's Lynn, went for a drink at the Maid's Head
at East Winch on the evening of 6 January 1830. It was not a particularly busy night and shortly before he left he noticed two
young men, who had been drawing attention from a few locals
in the pub that night; they just didn't like the look of them, particularly the one holding a great stick with a knobbed end. The
men left and when Rayner got outside, about ten minutes later,
he saw the men going down the high road. He turned down the
low road to make his way home to Middleton. As he proceeded
along the route, two men suddenly approached him from two
separate directions. One came and stopped the horse, whilst the
other man got onto the cart and began to beat Rayner with 'a
sharp thing' about half a yard long, and the other struck him with
a stick three times. They robbed him of all the money he was
carrying, a considerable sum from his bread round – one sovereign, about sixty or seventy shillings and some half pence – and
left him for dead. Rayner came to and knew he would recognise
the men again and swore, 'I know you and I'll have you.'

Rayner swore on oath before magistrates Sir W.J.H.B. Folkes and D. Gurney Esq. that his assailants had been James and William Brooks. Other witnesses were found and a warrant was issued for their arrest. Richard Sharpe, the Constable of Walsoken, was alerted to the whereabouts of the wanted men and set off with volunteers to Tilney All Saints to bring them in on 13 January. On seeing the constable the pair attempted to run away. They jumped a drainage ditch that was full of snow, but Constable Sharpe jumped after them and managed to get hold of James's coat, ripping of the lappet. One of the volunteers restrained him and soon both James and William Brooks were in custody, charged with robbery upon the King's Highway.

As they awaited trial, incarcerated at Norwich Castle, the two young men attempted a daring escape in the early hours of 26 February. Confined in the tall Bigod's Tower, James and William made it to the summit; nineteen-year-old William was first to lower himself by means of an improvised rope, which they had made from torn strips of blankets and the rug from their cell. The 'rope' gave way and Brooks fell 70ft. The fall did not kill him, however, and it was even remarked he appeared to have bounced – three yards the first time, two or three yards the second. He spoke as the warders recovered him but his thigh, pelvis, left arm and all the ribs

Bigod's Tower at Norwich Castle, c. 1900.

Prison hulks, *c.* 1860. The conditions were worse and the regime far harsher that their counterparts on land.

on his left side were broken, and a large tumour later formed in the hollow at the back of his head. Meanwhile, James was stuck at the top of the building and could go neither backwards nor forwards; he could only be removed with difficulty.

James Brooks was tried at the Norfolk Assizes, held at Thetford, in March 1830, while William, as Norwich Castle Prison Governor, John Johnson explained, 'was in a bad state' and was unable to attend. James was found guilty but the learned judge deferred sentence to see 'if there were any circumstances which would justify the sparing of his life.'

William Brooks was lucky to be alive but had been seriously disabled. When the Norfolk Assizes were held again in Norwich on 2 August 1830, he had to be brought from his cell on the back of one of the gaol warders, and supported himself on crutches through his trial. Found guilty of Highway Robbery, his sentence was deferred. Ultimately, both men evaded the gallows. James Brooks was sentenced to death, but the sentence was later commuted in favour of him being transported for life – he was one of the 216 convicts who departed British shores on 20 August 1830, aboard the *Clyde* bound for Van Diemen's Land. William also received a death sentence, which was commuted to life imprisonment, and he was removed to the prison hulk *Leviathan*, moored at Portsmouth, where he died in April 1881.

Chapter Two

Rebels and Rioters

Kett and his Rebels

On the weekend of 6 July 1549, many people from Wymondham and its surrounding villages gathered to celebrate the feast of the translation of St Thomas À Becket. The recent enclosures of land around the town proved to be an emotive subject and on the evening of Monday 8 July a group of townspeople tore down the enclosure fences of Mr Hobart of Morley, and then marched to Hethersett to destroy John Flowerdew's estate fences. Flowerdew bribed the mob to rip down Robert Kett's enclosures instead, but when they arrived at Kett's land, Kett went one better. He joined with the mob himself and helped them to tear down his own fences before leading them back Flowerdew's house, where they smashed his enclosures.

The rioters assembled again in Wymondham the following day and decided to march on to Norwich, with Robert Kett at their head and Kett's brother, William, at his right hand; their numbers greatly swelled by hundreds of protestors joining the march en route. When the rebels attempted to enter the city of Norwich on Wednesday 10 July, Mayor Thomas Codd and the

City Council refused them entry, fearing ideas of collaboration and spread of rebellion to the city itself. Sir Roger Wodehouse of Kimberley went to the rebels with carts containing beer and food to pacify them and urge them to disperse – the carts were seized and Wodehouse was taken prisoner. Staying outside of the city walls, the rebel force made camp on Mousehold and established a council comprising of a representative of the Norfolk and Suffolk Hundreds, from which the rebellion was born. Sitting under the later titled 'Oak of Reformation', the council issued warrants as 'the King's friends and deputies' to assemble food, cattle, weapons and people on Mousehold Heath. They also drew up a twenty-nine point charter of demands based almost entirely on righting the wrongs done to commoners over the previous decades. A Royal herald came to Kett's camp and read aloud terms for a general pardon. Kett refused, saying they had offended no laws and required no pardon. The herald denounced Kett as a traitor and any fiction of Royal sanction having been exposed, the Norwich authorities closed the city to the rebels. The following day the rebels stormed the city and met with little opposition. The city soon fell under rebel control and Mayor Codd and many of the City Fathers were taken prisoner.

A Royal Army, under the Marquis of Northampton, was despatched to the city and arrived on 31 July. The rebels fell back

Robert Kett holding 'court' on Mousehold, Norwich, 1549.

to Mousehold but returned again the same night; the fighting that ensued continued into the early hours, resulting in about 300 deaths, including Lord Sheffield.

A considerably larger force – estimated to have been comprised of up to 14,000 men, including mounted gentry and mercenaries – under the Earl of Warwick – arrived at the city on 23 August. Another herald was sent to Kett offering pardons but, was rejected again. Three days of intense fighting then commenced. The rebels took to heart the old Norfolk prophesy:

> The country Gnoffs, Hob, Dick and Hick
> With clubbes, and clouted shoon,
> Shall fill up Dussyndale
> With slaughtered bodies soon.

So, they went off to Dussin's Dale for their final battle. Unfortunately for them, the terrain was perfect for Warwick's cavalry, and with the mercenaries and the finest artillery that the Royal armouries could muster they smashed the rebel lines and claimed a bloody victory, with as many as 3,000 rebels slain.

The following morning the Earl of Warwick began to hear the cases of many of the prisoners his forces had captured. Justice was swift and many were executed on the city gallows outside the Magdalen Gates. Nine of the rebel leaders, including Miles, Kett's Master Gunner, were strung up on the 'Oak of Reformation', before being cut down again. Their bowels were then pulled out of their bodies and burned before their eyes, quickly followed by being beheaded and quartered. The heads and quarters were then set up on poles on the tops of the towers and gates of the city as a warning to all. A further forty-nine rebels were hanged on a specially erected gallows near the cross in the Market Place, thirty on the gallows outside the Magdalen Gates and many more in the towns and villages from whence the rebels came. In total, some 300 people are said to have suffered.

The worst fate awaited the Kett brothers. Robert and William were transported to the Tower of London, tried at the King's Bench and convicted of High Treason. Returned to the county, the Ketts were delivered to Sir William Windham, High Sheriff of

The commemorative plaque to Robert Kett on Norwich Castle, unveiled in 1949. It had been proposed by Alderman Fred Henderson, a former mayor of Norwich, who had been imprisoned in the castle for his part in the food riots of 1885.

Norfolk. On 9 December 1549, Robert Kett was paraded through the streets of Norwich, brought to the foot of the castle, drawn up to a gibbet by a rope fixed around his neck, erected onto the battlements and left hanging there 'till his body was entirely wasted'. His brother William suffered a similar sentence at Wymondham, his body being 'left to consume' in a gibbet cage suspended from the West Tower of Wymondham Abbey.

The Vitriolic Revolutionary

Richard Nockolds (also spelt Knockells) was one of the leading activists during the Norwich weaver's riots in January 1830. When the riots were put down by city officials and the streets kept quite by the use of mounted troops, Nockolds' fury festered and turned into a vicious attack upon John Wright, one of the principal master manufacturers of Norwich. Leaping out of the shadows on St Faith's Lane, Nockolds threw Vitriol (Sulphuric Acid) in Wright's face. Dreadfully injured and partially blinded by the corrosive liquid, Mr Wright discharged his pistol at his

A typical provincial riot in the nineteenth century: If identified and brought to justice, ringleaders and active participants would face stiff penalties for such actions.

assailant, but Nockolds escaped and was not recognised by Wright. The attack drew a great deal of publicity and despite a reward of £100 being offered to anyone identifying Wright's assailant, Nockolds was not given up.

In November 1830, the voices of disquiet rose again, but this time from farm labourers after so many of them had been rendered superfluous by the new harvesting machinery. Activists like Nockolds mustered labourers into rioting mobs, who set about breaking the machinery and setting fire to haystacks at a number of locations throughout the county.

Guildhall, Norwich,

DECEMBER 4th, 1830.

The Mayor and Magistrates consider it to be a paramount duty which they owe to their Sovereign and their Country at this moment of general disturbance, to declare that, whilst in common with the rest of their Fellow Citizens, they are on the one hand ready to do all which sympathy and benevolence can suggest for the relief of distressed operatives in this populous place, so on the other hand it is their full determination to act with the promptitude, decision, and vigour, which circumstances imperatively demand, in prohibiting tumultuous assemblies, and suppressing riotous proceedings, in opposing every kind of open outrage, and actively endeavouring to detect secret attacks, on either Person or Property.

The Mayor and Magistrates are anxious to impress on the minds of their Fellow Citizens, that persons who are guilty of these lawless proceedings, are liable on conviction to suffer Death, and that the loss incurred by Individuals by the destruction of their Property must be paid by the Public, and will consequently tend to the increase of the County Rate.—Taking the present occasion therefore to acknowledge and applaud the zeal of numerous respectable Individuals, who in voluntary compliance with the summons already issued, have meritoriously come forward as Special Constables, the Mayor and Magistrates renew their call on every well-disposed Person, capable of rendering assistance, to enrol himself on the same list, being firmly resolved upon an organized and efficient employment of the Civil power, supported, if there should be need, with such other aid as is authorized by Law, for the speedy restoration of public tranquillity.

W. SIMPSON,
TOWN CLERK.

In 1830, the authorities in Norwich appealed for citizens to volunteer to become Special Constables in the event of further riots.

The execution of rebel leader Richard Nockolds, as depicted on the broadside sold after his execution at Norwich Castle in April 1831.

At the 1831 Lent Assizes, Richard Nockolds and three alleged accomplices appeared, accused of setting fire to haystacks, the property of farmer William Blake of Swanton Abbott. They were found not guilty of this crime but were immediately charged with the same offence on Richard Ducker's farm. It was proved that Nockolds had left notes at the scene of the crime; his hand-writing matched and the notebooks showing the indentations of the messages were presented in court. In the face of this evidence Nockolds stood little chance of evading the charge, and he alone was found guilty and sentenced to death. Nockolds was penitent; he confessed to throwing vitriol in the face of Mr Wright and pleaded forgiveness for his wife and young family. Nockolds was executed in front of Norwich Castle on 9 April 1831. After hanging for the usual hour his family were allowed to take his body away to their cottage, where they exhibited it; a small charge was made to view his body and a contemporary report concluded that 'a considerable sum of money was in this way raised for his widow.'

Chapter Three

Armed Siege

The Siege of Northumberland Street

At about 6.30 a.m. on 21 February 1889, PC James Southgate was walking homeward along Northumberland Street after a night pounding the city beat, no doubt looking forward to a sit down by a warm fire, mug of cocoa and a well-earned sleep, when he encountered Joseph Betts. Betts was a character well known to Norwich City Police as a 'rowdy' – known for stirring up trouble with his drink-fuelled outbursts. Betts had been brought before the magistrates in 1883, after sending threatening letters to the Bishop of Norwich and his boss, one of the city's largest and most benevolent employers – Mr J. J. Colman, the mustard and starch manufacturer of Carrow Works. The Bishop had refused to press charges but the threat to murder Mr Colman if he did not distribute 'last year's balance' among his workers was taken seriously, and Betts was sent down for twelve months with hard labour and ordered to keep the peace on his release.

Betts confronted PC Southgate, cursing and muttering something about false charges levelled against him by the police. Before Southgate knew what was happening, Betts had drawn a revolver and had fired it at Southgate. Betts was clearly possessed with a great rage and his aim was such that the bullet actually ripped through the constable's greatcoat between his arm and body, grazing the officer's arm. Seeing Betts preparing to fire again, the constable was now wide awake, his heartbeat thumping in his chest, and he made his escape. Southgate summoned the assistance of PC Clarke and PC Holland and returned to Northumberland Street, where they discovered Betts had locked himself in his house, had taken position in his bedroom, and was threatening to shoot anyone who dared to approach. Word of the situation was despatched to Norwich Police headquarters in the Guildhall and the Chief Constable, Robert Hitchman, was briefed on the situation. The police were soon faced with the added challenge of controlling the crowds, who had gathered to watch the incident as they passed on their way to work. As news of the siege spread all over the city, more and more curious people and press arrived on Northumberland Street.

Magistrates were approached to grant a warrant for the arrest of Betts and, by noon, Inspector Guiett and a team of officers were present to execute it. Calls for admission were met with a verbal tirade and it was made quite clear that Betts had no respect for the law or any warrant. Inspector Guiett bravely took it upon himself to obtain a ladder and put it up against the bedroom window. He had hardly set foot on the bottom rung when Betts leant out of the window and fired blindly at the officer. A bullet hit the peak of the Inspector's cap and traversed across his forehead, breaking the flesh. Removed from the scene for his wound to be dressed, it was soon discovered that the Inspector had miraculously escaped any serious wound. Fired up by the treatment of their Inspector, the remaining policemen forced the front door open and made it up the stairs to Bett's bedroom, only to discover that he had barricaded the door. PC Airey and Sergeant Hall attempted to force the door and managed to get it open a few inches, but were soon rebuffed with an unnervingly near shot from Betts as Hall attempted to peer through. Police officers occupied the rooms of the house but thought it best to let Betts calm down for a while and simply sit out the siege. No further attempts were made to force the door.

At 2.45 p.m. the city's Chief Constable arrived in a horse-drawn cab, accompanied by PC Mickleburgh. Making his way through the crowd and police line, and wisely observing a high

Members of the Norwich City Police, c. 1885. (Norfolk Constabulary Archive)

wall where he could dive for cover, Chief Constable Hitchman bravely strode out in front of the house to address Betts personally. Betts instantly appeared at the window and, maniacally laughing, he pointed the revolver at Hitchman. Sensing the 'power' the weapon gave him he stayed at the window, waving the weapon around, revelling in driving the Chief Constable to take cover and the fearful gasp and recoil of the crowd.

Detective Rushmer was outside the bedroom door inside the house and managed to draw Betts in from the window and open negotiations. He soon discovered that Betts was willing to give himself up, but only to a solicitor. Unable to procure such a man at short notice, a reporter named Hook was asked to fill the role and was assured that no harm would be allowed to come to him (how they could guarantee this is not known). No doubt game for an exclusive, the reporter agreed and was introduced through the barricaded door as 'Mr Sadd', the solicitor. Betts requested the solicitor be taken outside onto the street in front of the bedroom window and shown to him. After Betts fixed 'Mr Sadd' firmly in his gaze, the mock solicitor assured Betts he would be taken care of. Betts agreed to surrender. The ladder was returned to the window and he descended to the ground, where the police closed in to restrain Betts before removing him, by cab, to the police station – much to the cheers and applause of the crowd.

Betts stood trial and was sentenced to fifteen years penal servitude, but was later found to be 'of unsound mind' and was removed to Broadmoor Criminal Lunatic Asylum.

Chapter Four

Bodysnatching

The human body – how it was constructed and functioned – had been surrounded by mystery and fascination since ancient history. Until the eighteenth century, any attempt by a medical man to open the body cavity of a living human being would mean almost certain death for the patient. Out of enlightened thought, experiments and, above all, detailed examination and dissection of cadavers, medical knowledge was advancing by leaps and bounds by the early years of the nineteenth century. Bodies of executed felons, suicides and unclaimed bodies recovered from rivers were all fair game for the dissection table, but such legitimate supplies did not meet, by any means, the demands of the medical schools. So, a sinister new chain of supply emerged – bodysnatching!

This act was usually committed by gangs in the dark of the night; the glow of the moon and lanterns lighting the way to recently filled graves, digging down to the coffin, removing the body and carting it away for resale to the surgeon's men. This was no minor operation; groups of bodysnatchers, otherwise known as 'resurrectionists' or 'resurrection men', appear to have operated across most of Great Britain. Norfolk-born London surgeon, Astley Cooper, (later appointed Professor of Anatomy to the Royal College of Surgeons; personal physician to the Monarch; and a baronet) took grim satisfaction in telling a House of Commons investigation

Surgeon and anatomist Sir Astley Paston Cooper (1768-1841).

An executed prisoner on display to the public in a surgeon's hall, after the initial procedures of the anatomists.

there was 'no person, whatever his situation might be, whose body, after death, I cannot obtain.'

In December 1827, 'resurrectionist' activities were detected in Great Yarmouth. George Beck, a local baker, was concerned to find his recently buried wife's grave apparently disturbed. Further investigation confirmed his worst fears – the body had been stolen. Several other recently bereaved families also had their worst fears confirmed upon investigation – around twenty graves were found to have been tampered with. The bodysnatching gang may have received warning of the discovery of their nocturnal activities and slipped away into the darkness, but their leader, Thomas Vaughan, had 'behaved ill to a young woman to whom he passed himself off as a bachelor' and the wronged woman informed the authorities of what she knew of Vaughan's bodysnatching activites and the rest of the gang were soon identified and their base, a rented house near St Nicholas Church (and its graveyard) in Row 6, then known as Browne's or Rackham's Row,

St Nicholas Church and graveyard in the early nineteenth century.

was discovered. Following this grim discovery the row was known as Snatchbody Row.

Among the other gang members were father and son team, William and Robert Barber. The son, Robert, turned King's Evidence in a plea for leniency and told how he and his father robbed the graves, packed bodies in boxes and sent them by train to London, naming Surgeon Astley Cooper as the final recipient of the corpses. The most adept member of the gang was a tall, strong Irishman named Murphy, who handled the bodies. He had been paid £12 12s each for at least four of the bodies from Yarmouth.

Astley Cooper and his fellow London surgeons did not forsake their resurrection men. A legal representative was sent to act on behalf of Vaughan, for the grand sum, in those days, of £14. Vaughan was even granted by his surgeon employers 10 shillings a week for the twenty-six weeks he was in confinement. Murphy was also well treated and for his defence at trial, the not inconsiderable amount of £160 was also paid by the surgeons.

Luckily for Vaughan, the relatively new crime of bodysnatching had no specific legislature against it; to remove a body from a grave was not strictly illegal and could only be treated as a misdemeanour, for which he was found guilty and the maximum sentence of six months in the House of Correction was meted

Bodysnatchers labouring at their grim business by moonlight in the early nineteenth century.

out. To apply a more robust approach to bodysnatching, the law soon found a loophole whereby the 'resurrectionists' could be prosecuted, not for the theft of the body but rather the act of stealing the shroud in which the cadaver had been dressed. An intriguing footnote is to be found in the ultimate fate of Vaughan. After his release, while in Plymouth, he had not learned his lesson and fell foul of the law by 'appropriating the clothes in which a dead body had been wrapped.' Successfully prosecuted for the felony, Vaughan was transported to Australia.

Chapter Five

Arson

A Flash and a Scare

In the late eighteenth and early nineteenth century, firing stacks –
an act often referred to as 'incendiarism' – had become a common
form of rural protest and became highly prevalent in times of
hardship or scarcity of food. To keep this activity in check, stiff
penalties were handed down upon those who commited such
crimes and on occasion some would be made examples of, as a
warning and a reminder to all of the full rigour of the law in cases
of arson. Noah Peak (aged forty) of Shelfanger, and George Fortis
(twenty-nine) of North Lopham, were both ex-soldiers who had
served in the Peninsula War and both had been present on the
field of Waterloo. Implicated in the confessions of two accomplices, both men were charged on the oath of Diss farmer, John
Kent, with having been accessories to setting fire to three of his
haystacks on 25 February 1822. Accomplice William Baker turned
King's Evidence and told the damning story of how Peak had
invited him to come and have some food and how he had accompanied Peak and Fortis as they fired the stacks that same evening.
Tried and found guilty at the assizes, both Peak and Fortis made

their confessions from the condemned cell. Peak confessed to the chaplain that it was he who had entered the stack yard with the 'live tarf' and placed it in the straw to start the fire. Asked for his motive, he said he wanted to send a 'flash and a scare' to alarm the local farmers into making a more generous allowance to the poor.

Peak and Fortis were sent to the gallows on Castle Hill on 13 April 1822. Both men were permitted to address the crowd. Fortis gave an eloquent address urging others to learn from his errors, while Peak urged all to take note of what Fortis had said then went on to declare that some of the witnesses against them had 'sworn wrongfully'. It was reported that, after a prompting from the chaplain, both men acknowledged the justice of their sentence before being 'tied up and the caps drawn over their faces, while they were distinctly and audibly repeating after the chaplain, a short prayer, the platform fell and they died, almost without a struggle.'

A Reckless Love of Mischief

Twenty-year-old James Clarke lived in a cottage with his mother in the rural village of Buxton. On the night of 20 January 1835 he called in on neighbour, Ben Dawson, saying he had been to The Lion public house where he had seen his mother, who was tired after a long day washing, and had asked him to go home to light a fire for her, which required a light from an ember to start it. Dawson's fire was nearly burnt out, but he said that Clarke was welcome to have a rake around and that there should have been enough to get a light. Dawson left the room and when he returned Clarke was gone. Moments later, Robert Page and Gideon Fitt were passing along the road near John Bambridge's wheat stack on Bartram's Meadow when their attention was caught by a glint of light through the hedge. Wondering what the light could be, the men went to investigate and saw a man they firmly believed to be Clarke with the flame. They then observed him take a sheaf from the stack, put a light in its place, put the sheaves down on the fire, before the stack suddenly burst into flames. Clarke then made off along the side of a hedge. Despite both Fitt and Page deciding to go after the incendiary, they lost him in the darkness. The alarm was raised for help to extinguish the fire and many people came to assist, including James Clarke, but the stack was consumed by the flames. Curiously, it was only some time later, when Clarke had to secure regular employment in Buxton and had gone to King's Lynn to follow his long-term intention of going to sea, that Page and Fitt told their story. Upon receipt of this statement George Rayson, the constable of Buxton, set off in pursuit of Clarke who had, by that time, sailed up to Sunderland, found a position on a vessel and was awaiting his ship to sail. The constable traced Clarke to his lodging house and he was taken from his bed that night and returned over 300 miles back to Norwich Castle, where he would await his appearance before the Norfolk Assizes.

At his trial Clarke, admitted the stack was situated about 100 yards from his own house but he declared his innocence, claiming he had gone to the area to gather kindling for his mother's fire, saw the light near the stack, and ran there to help extinguish the resulting fire. Clarke's defence made much of Page and Fitt's failure to reveal what they knew until quite some time after the event, but to no avail, the jury believed he was guilty of the deed and Clarke was sent to the gallows. After his condemnation, Clarke was left to his own reflections in his cell for half an hour; when the chaplain entered he found the man in tears. Clarke did not deny his guilt; indeed he confessed to the crime, but he vehemently denied any part in any of the other seven similar offences that had occurred around the area of his village. He then took the pains to point out that he bore no grudge against Mr Bambridge, admitting that he had always treated him with kindness and that he had committed the offence on a whim, partly under the influence of drink, but mostly from a 'reckless love of mischief'. Executed upon Norwich Castle Hill on 18 April 1835, James Clarke was the last man to be hanged in Norfolk for arson.

Incendiarism in Norfolk

In August 1844, no less than seven cases of incendiarism were brought before the Norfolk Summer Assizes. Four people had been committed to prison and had awaited their appearance at the

The Swaffham Petty Sessions court building, where a number of the 'incediaries' made their first appearance before being sent to the assizes.

assizes at Swaffham, namely George Garrod (sixteen), committed on 15 May for setting fire to a stable at Didlington; William Baker (twenty-nine), for setting fire to a stack of wheat at Foulden on 4 May, the property of John Richardson; Matthew Barnes (eleven), for setting fire to a stack of wheat, the property of John and William Wetherell on 20 May; and William Nichols (twenty-three) for setting fire to a stack of straw at Feltwell, the property of Jonathan Flower. Anna Maria Frary (forty) had been committed from Wymondham for setting fire to a cowshed owned by her uncle, Samuel Cooke, and the last two came from Norwich Gaol; Henry Rowing (eighteen), for setting fire to some growing furze at Shipdam, the property of the Revd B. Barker, and Richard Potter (twelve) for setting fire to a stack of straw, the property of Nathaniel Nunn of North Lopham.

Young George Garrod was fortunate as the grand jury ignored the bill against him, and no bill was found against William Baker, Matthew Barnes or William Nichols. Anna Maria Frary had quarrelled with her uncle and he had taken a summons out upon her on the Monday previous to the fire. Witnesses stated that as a result of the summons, Frary had sworn revenge and had made a number of threats to 'burn the place down.' She had been seen entering the cowshed and just a few minutes later the place was ablaze. Frary insisted she was innocent throughout her trial and continued to do so as sentence was passed. Neither the jury nor the learned judge believed her; however, he was inclined to show some mercy. In consideration of the fact that she was a married woman with five children he did not sentence her to transportation, as he was entitled to do for such an offence, instead he gave her two years imprisonment with hard labour.

Henry Rowing had been found guilty of firing the furze but the judge believed he 'required a more mitigated sentence than all preceded' because the furze he had set ablaze was not a large district but one of limited extent; no crops had been destroyed, it had been easily extinguished, and was 'attended with the most trifling expense.' He was sentenced to three months imprisonment with hard labour for his crime. Young Richard Potter was the last of the incendiaries to be sentenced. He had pleaded guilty to the charge against him, the judge believed that he was sincerely sorry for what he had done and, in consideration of his young age, he was sent down for two years with hard labour.

He Got His Wish

On the night of 21 June 1850, herring fish hawker Timothy Burch (twenty-four) was at the Crown Inn at Kenninghall in a 'froshy' state when he saw a blind nut dealer who he heard had been transported. Burch, who was animated by his chance encounter, spoke to the blind man, and enquired about the country he had been transported to and what sort of food he had been served there. The reply was, 'Oh, the rations is three and a half pounds of meat per week.' This seemed to appeal to Burch – clearly he had not asked about the hard labour that went with it – and he replied, 'Is it? Then if I didn't fire five stacks three weeks ago at Tebbingham [Tuddenham] and I'm blessed if I won't fire every stack on my way home tonight!' He promptly bought a box of lucifer matches and set off on his way home. Beginning at the farm of Thomas Womack at Kenninghall, where he set fire to a wheat stack, Burch went on to commit no less than seven distinct acts of incendiarism that marked his progress along the five miles between the pub and his cottage. The morning light revealed tracks, almost to his door, many of which proved to be perfect matches to the impressions left by Burch's boots across cropped and fallowed fields, as well as the breaks through the hedges he had made as he passed from one to another. Brought before Mr Baron Alderson at the assizes, the evidence was damning and the jury had little hesitation in returning a guilty verdict. Burch was sentenced to transportation for life, with the warning from the judge that 'he would not find the life of a man transported for such a diabolical series of outrages on society to be by any means an agreeable one.'

The Tragic Tale of Harriet Kettle

Harriet Kettle of Cranworth had been a pauper in the Mitford and Launditch Union Workhouse at Gressenhall since the age of six, after her mother died and her father was unable to care for her. When Kettle became a young woman she left the workhouse and went to seek employment in Norwich, but ended up falling in with the wrong crowd and worked as a prostitute for a few

The Mitford and Launditch Union Workhouse at Gressenhall, *c.* 1905.

years. She returned to the Gressenhall workhouse but was a difficult inmate. She attacked the workhouse master and was sent to Walsingham Bridewell, but concerns for her state of mind caused her to be sent to the County Lunatic Asylum at Thorpe in 1856. While at the asylum she was described as 'violent,' 'disobedient' and a 'suicidal lunatic'.

Obtaining a discharge from the asylum she returned again to the workhouse, but in 1859 she attempted to set fire to the building. Indicted at the Norfolk Summer Assizes, she was found to be insane and was ordered to be detained at Her Majesty's pleasure. In March 1860, she was brought up for trial before Mr Justice Williams. After the case had been proved, the master of the asylum and the surgeon of the gaol – in answer to questions from the judge – both gave their opinion that the prisoner was not insane and that her conduct was the result of the passionate dislike that Kettle had formed for the matron of the workhouse; Harriet had fought with her in the dining hall and been sent to the punishment room – she had set fire to her bed and furniture in a fit of rage. After some consideration, the foreman of the jury said, 'We believe she did it with a bad intent and that she was of sane mind when she did it.' Kettle was sent down for eighteen months with hard labour. After serving her sentence, she was returned to the County Lunatic Asylum and was released from there in 1864.

Chapter Six

Vitriol and Plaster

Looking over the annals of crime in Norfolk, some unusual weapons have been used over the years. Here are two examples of these crimes.

Oil of vitriol, also known as sulphuric acid, has featured in a number of cases as an offensive weapon used by both men and women; in this case from 1882 it was the choice of a woman scorned.

Around 7.10 p.m. on Saturday, 7 January 1882, William Cooper was walking towards St Benedict's Gates where he was to meet a young lady, when Charlotte Ransome came running up behind him and threw the contents of a basin in his face. Cooper's face instantly began to suffer a burning sensation and he rubbed his face with his hands, but it only made the burning intensify. He began to panic, called out for help and was taken to the nearby Barn Tavern. Once inside, his face was bathed, a doctor was called and Cooper was removed to his home, where his face was dressed.

The attack was a matter for the police; Charlotte Ransome (aged twenty-two) was arrested and the case was brought before the Norwich Guildhall Sessions on Saturday 14 January. The right side of Cooper's face and his neck had suffered extensive burns from the acid and it was remarked in the press that his face and head 'presented a frightful spectacle.' In cross-examination,

The Norwich Guildhall, c. 1905

Cooper admitted he had been to Ransome's house on Bailey Street, Heigham, on 'one or two occasions', that she had his portrait, and, about eleven months previously, she had told him she was pregnant. It seems there had been a suggestion Cooper had recommended Ransome to 'take a certain mixture' (as an abortifacient) and that she had also given him money, although she would not say in court what it was for; indeed, she refused to make any statement and was committed by the magistrates to take her trial at the next Norfolk Assizes, where she was found guilty of the crime and sentenced to twelve months imprisonment.

Our second case involves one of the most unusual weapons used in a Norfolk crime. Thirty-eight-year-old Samuel Horth was a married man with a wife and children who was employed as a porter by Thomas Bunn, a corn merchant in Southtown, Great Yarmouth. Horth would usually report to his master's house in the morning to clean the family boots and shoes and assist the house servant, Ann Proudfoot, in household work. Horth and Proudfoot became intimate and as a result she fell pregnant. Proudfoot broached the subject with Horth and told him that she would require some money for her confinement; he replied that he 'would think about it.'

Horth arranged to meet Proudfoot on the Denes at 8 p.m. on 14 October 1852, to discuss the matter further. They walked as they talked and when they came to Tooley's Mill corner they lay down on the ground for a time. As they were getting up again Horth produced what appeared to be a pitch plaster, clapped it over her mouth and attempted to hold her down. Proudfoot managed to struggle free and stand up, tore off the plaster and ran off screaming 'Murder!' Horth caught up with her and renewed his attempt to apply the plaster and made a ferocious attack upon her. He beat her brutally about the head and body and knocked her front teeth in. He then left her insensible on the ground. Proudfoot's cries of murder had been heard about 200 yards away in the Northumberland Arms Inn and a number of the customers came running. They found her on the ground, with the remnants of pitch over her mouth and the plaster stuck to her gown. When she recovered herself enough to speak, she named Horth as the person who had committed the outrage.

Horth lived only a short distance away at No. 5, Row 50, and when the police arrived they found him sitting at home with his family smoking his pipe. Horth claimed he had been at home all evening. However, the coming of the morning light revealed signs of a violent struggle where Proudfoot had been found, as well as a brace that resembled the one usually worn by Horth. A search of Horth's house also revealed an iron pot of pitch; the same sort that the plaster had been made from and which had been found on Proudfoot – Horth's hand was also found to be stained with the same pitch. Horth was arrested and brought before the Norfolk Assizes in March 1853. Witnesses testified to Horth's previously good character before the jury retired for twenty minutes and returned a verdict, finding Horth guilty of attempting to put a plaster over the face of Proudfoot, but not with intent to murder her. He was sentenced to eighteen months imprisonment.

Chapter Seven

At Her Majesty's Pleasure

The Carlton Rode Killing

Forty-one-year-old Richard Scott was a man known to have occasional irrational and violent outbursts; some said it ran in his family. On the morning of Friday, 31 July 1829, Scott had entered the Queen's Head pub at Bunwell and alarmed the landlady by his wild looks and violent behaviour. Striking his hand with great force on the table in the kitchen, he exclaimed, 'Look, there is the devil; I can see him!' On leaving the pub, Scott returned to his home at Carlton Rode, where he repeated similar acts of frenzy. The following morning Scott went to see Mr. J. Dodd, a surgeon at New Buckenham, to be bled; this was a common enough medical procedure at the time to release some of the blood pressing on the brain that was believed to cause headaches and mental disturbances. It didn't seem to do much good. On his return home after the procedure, Scott encountered eighty-year-old James Freeman, who was walking along the road, following his discharge from the County Gaol after a short prison term for a minor offence. Upon seeing Freeman, Scott cried out, 'Here is the devil!' and instantly dealt him a blow with his fist, sending Freeman to the ground. Scott then leapt upon Freeman and, picking up the old man's stick, set about him with it in a frenzied attack, fracturing his skull 'in a dreadful manner'. He continued to hit him until he seemed to tire, then he stood up and calmly walked towards his own house.

The incident brought people nearby running to the scene; Scott gave up the murder weapon and offered no resistance. Summoned to the scene, surgeon Mr H. Howard of New Buckenham saw the bloody body of Freeman, and confirmed that he had died from the wounds inflicted upon his skull. Scott's behaviour after the attack was in complete contrast, for he sat in a tranquil state as he waited the arrival of the constable, although it was remarked that his exertions had caused the vein through which he had been bled to 'burst out afresh' and that he had been reduced to a state of weakness through loss of blood. While Scott was held in his cottage during the afternoon and evening, he had a number of wild outbursts of speech and swore, at length, that the devil had been harassing him about where he had been mowing with his scythe; sometimes when he took a stroke or two there was the old man at his heels; when he went a dozen yards to get rid of him, the old man was at his heels again. Scott also repeated, as statement, that he had seen that evening 'one of the most beautiful young men that were ever seen with the eyes.' Scott claimed that after his vision, he turned and saw the old man Freeman 'with his teeth as long as his fingers.' After he had shown the length of his teeth, Scott promptly got a hot potato and slapped it into his mouth. He then told a tale of how, while moving, he had also mowed across the back of a very fine pair of ducks, 'till I mowed their tails off'. The coroner's inquest returned a verdict of wilful murder against Scott and he was committed to Norwich Castle.

Brought before the Norfolk Assizes on Tuesday, 18 August 1829, Scott appeared 'perfectly composed' when placed at the bar and pleaded 'not guilty' to the charge of murder brought against him. In his summing up, Mr Justice Park said there could be no doubt that Scott had been in a frenzy and 'the law empowered the jury to find a special verdict of acquittal on the ground that he was insane and would be kept in custody for the future.' The jury returned their verdict accordingly and Scott was detained 'until Her Majesty's pleasure be known'.

Sins of the Father

Thirty-five-year-old William Frost was a God-fearing family man who lived in Whitwell, near Reepham, with his wife Martha and their four children Harriet (five), Charlotte (three), Eliza (eighteen months) and ten-week-old Louisa. He was a respectable, sober and steady man who had enjoyed employment as a journeyman tanner for Mr Robert Leamon for the past fourteen years. Frost had been a member of the religious fraternity known as the 'Ranters' and had sometimes officiated as a preacher. Subsequently he had become an active members of the 'Revivalists' or Primitive Methodists, where he had become a preacher of some repute, however, it had been noted that over recent times had had been 'under the influence of a gloomy set of fanaticism.'

On Monday, 8 April 1844, Frost's wife left her husband having breakfast with the elder children in the cottage to call upon Mrs Watkins, a neighbour, to collect a shilling that she was owed. All seemed well and normal – just another day. Finding the neighbour was not there Mrs Frost returned home and, after a short conversation with another neighbour, went inside. Suddenly, a terrible cry was heard and Mrs Frost screamed 'Oh, my children!' On hearing this, Sarah Allen, who lived in the adjoining cottage, ran around to see what had happened. On arrival, she found Mrs Frost unable to speak and saw young Eliza lying dead in the pantry, her head battered and covered in blood. Sarah then went upstairs and discovered Harriet and Charlotte, also with their heads battered and bloody, laying dead on the floor; all this time William Frost was sitting by the fireside in the kitchen. Mrs Allen went over to Frost and took hold of him, saying, 'Oh man! What have you done?' He made no reply. Mrs Allen then noticed the baby, Louisa, head down in an earthenware vessel partly filled with water. She lifted the child up, only to find that she too was dead.

Other neighbours had followed Mrs Allen and very soon the cottage had become crowded, but Frost continued to say nothing to any of them. His boss, Mr Leamon, came in and talked directly to Frost, asking, 'Did you ever think of doing this before?' Frost clearly thought for a while then said, 'Yes, for some time past.'

Leamon then asked if he had thought of destroying himself. Frost also replied 'Yes' and went on to say that he believed that if he 'made off' with his children, that they would go to heaven.

Samuel Parker, an Inspector of Police residing at Reepham, arrived, arrested Frost and put him in handcuffs. Searching for the murder weapon, he found a large hammer that had clearly been recently washed but still showed some traces of blood on the head. Parker showed it to Frost and asked, 'Is this the one you committed that act with?' Frost simply replied 'Yes' and he confessed to washing it too. When taken into custody, Frost voluntarily stated how he had committed the dreadful deeds. 'Poor things,' he said of his children, 'I killed the two young ones first and then I took the two eldest upstairs and dashed them down with a hammer. I wished to put them out of their misery, poor things.' After this he raised his hands to heaven and cried out, 'Glory to God! My sins are pardoned and I am forgiven for my crimes and am going to heaven.'

It is interesting to note that during the 1850s, instances of parents killing children had been known to occur because of straightened circumstances, but the newspaper reports of Frost were keen to point out that, 'It did not appear that the prisoner was in any dread of want which could induce him to make away with his children. On the contrary, he was in comfortable circumstances for one of his station in life.'

The County Coroner, Mr Pilgrim, empanelled a jury from different parishes and the inquest was conducted the following morning at The Falgate public house. The jury were taken to the Frosts' cottage to examine the children's bodies and were all shocked at the deplorable spectacle that confronted them. When questioned at the hearing, Frost claimed he could not recall much about the incident beyond confirming a statement he had given to the police with the words, 'I have nothing more to say, I slayed my children, the two below stairs first.' The Coroner observed that he considered this to be one of the most horrible cases he had ever known and that in his opinion there could be 'little or no doubt as to the guilty party.' The jury almost instantly returned a verdict of wilful murder against Frost, and the Coroner issued his warrant for the committal of Frost to the County Gaol to await trial at the next Norfolk Assizes.

Some of the jury wanted to add an opinion to the verdict:

> That it was feared the said William Frost committed the act under the excitement of certain religious impressions, unfortunately prevalent in the neighbourhood, of the mischievous tendency of which many could not refrain from expressing their decided approbation.

Other members thought it better to have the opinion omitted from the verdict, which was agreed, but it was still published in the press.

Frost was transported to Norwich Castle the same evening under the escort of two policemen. He occupied himself for most of the journey by singing hymns and psalms. Brought before the Norfolk Assizes in August 1844, when called upon to plead,

---

TRIAL OF
William FROST
(AND JUDGES' ADDRESS)
FOR THE
BARBAROUS MURDERS
OF HIS FOUR DEAR CHILDREN

William FROST

William Frost, aged 35, was indicted on the coroner's inquisition for having, on the 8th day of April last, at Whitwell, murdered Harriet Frost 5 years old, Charlotte Frost 3, Eliza Frost 18 months, & Louisa Frost, only 10 weeks old, his children.

The case created a great degree of excitement when it came on for trial, as a more horrible occurrence had never been known, in this or in any other county.

Mr. Evans prosecuted, and Mr. Dasent defended the prisoner.

The prisoner was placed at the bar amid a dead silence. He sighed heavily [when arraigned, but had a very sullen and steadfast expression of countenance.

When called upon to plead to the indictment, he said, "I may be guilty enough in the sight of the world; but am not guilty in the sight of God."—The Clerk of the Arraigns then arraigned him on the Coroner's Inquisition, and said, 'how say you, are you guilty or not guilty.'—Pris. I do not understand that term.

The Clerk of the Arraigns.—The Coroner's Jury have returned a verdict of Wilful Murder against you, to which you must plead guilty or not guilty.—Prisoner. I shall not plead guilty of wilful murder.

This was taken as a plea of "Not Guilty."

Mr. Evans said, that it was his duty to state to them the means by which he thought to bring home the offence to the prisoner at the bar. As to the question whether he did or did not do the deed, there could be no or but very little doubt. The only difficulty would be as to the state of his mind, at the time he committed it. They would find, that for many years before he committed this dreadful act, he had resided at Whitwell, in this county. He was a married man, with several children, and he (Mr. E.) was bound to say in fairness to the prisoner that up to this time he had borne a most irreproachable character. The eldest child was about five years old, the youngest an infant not more than ten weeks old. One of the next door neighbours went into his house on the morning in question; the prisoner was sitting by the fire, with his wife in the room in the utmost distress, in consequence of the four children having been murdered. The people who went in naturally asked him how he came to do such a deed, to which he made no reply. His master Mr. [Lennon] very shortly arrived, and he thought it right to put certain questions to him, not with any desire to make the prisoner criminate himself, but with a view to ascertain something as to the state of his mind.

Robert Lennon sworn,—the prisoner was in my employment. He has been in my employ for 14 years, principally in the tannery. I had heard of his being unwell a fortnight or three weeks before this happened, and went to his home. He asked me if I would give him a little medicine, which I did, as I had frequently done before. He feared he had a rupture coming. He had been away from work four days in the week previous; in consequence of what I had heard I went to his house on the Monday about 10 in the morning; I observed the two eldest children in the manner described; I saw the prisoner sitting by a table handcuffed; a policeman, named Parker, was there when I got there; I said Frost, what can you have been thinking of to have committed this horrible deed? He made no reply at all, & somebody said to me, it is of no use asking him any questions for he will answer no one. Then seeing the house crowded I said to Parker, "clear the house Parker, and I think he will speak to me."—

I repeated the same question, and he merely pressed his face all this time was close to the table. I then said, " Frost you are the last man I should have thought capable of such business." He said " No," Then I said "Did you expect, by butchering your innocent children, in this way, you would be the means of getting them to heaven?" He said, "I hope so," I said, " Had you any thoughts of destroying yourself?" "I had," At that time the policeman produced a hammer to the prisoner, and I asked Frost, "if that was the hammer with which he killed the children?" Frost said it was. I asked Frost, "if it was true, as Parker said, that the hammer was fresh washed?" He said it was.

Mr. Crosse said he had examined the prisoner a few days after his admission, and repeatedly since. The result of those conferences led him to consider him of unsound mind. During his early visits the prisoner was very sullen but rational, and he particularly avoided entering on the subject of the murder of his children. He detailed to witness the circumstance that [distressed] his mind, as to falling off from his religious duties, and the circumstances under which he attempted to resume them but failed.

The Learned Judge in summing up, said, the prisoner at the bar was indicted for the highest offence but one, of which any human being could be guilty; and of course he need not say, that the case demanded the most serious and anxious attention. There could be no doubt the prisoner at the bar was the cause of the death of his children; that fact was placed beyond all doubt. Not only by the evidence it appeared, that a neighbouring woman saw his wife go out, and upon her returning, heard her utter a violent shriek; and when she went in she found the children all put to death. Consequently the prisoner, and nobody else but him, must have done it. there having been no one else in the house. It had however been stated, that the great question was, whether on this evidence the jury were of opinion that the prisoner at the bar was, at the time of his committing the act, insane ? The Learned Judge would not, however, leave this point in that generality of expression. He agreed in the distinction made by Mr. Crosse, that it was not a just definition to say a person was insane because he did not know right from wrong. The question was, whether the prisoner understood the quality of the particular act...—whether or not the prisoner, when he put his four children to death, knew that he was wrong? Not whether he knew whether it was right or wrong to calumniate his neighbourhood or perjure himself; but whether he put his children to death in the belief that he was doing right? That was the point for the consideration of the jury. They heard the opinion of the medical men, and no doubt that opinion was a fact in the case to be taken into consideration, but it was for the jury to say whether the other facts of the case might not over-balance the weight of this opinion. The Learned Judge further summed up the evidence at great length with extreme minuteness.

The jury, after a short consultation returned a verdict "of GUILTY," but first the act was done whilst he was in a state of insanity.

The Clerk of the arraigns said, then you will say he is not guilty on account of insanity.

The trial commenced at eleven and ended at six o'clock.

Printed by Robert Walker, St. Martin at Oak, Norwich.

The broadside sold after the trial of William Frost in April 1844.

Frost said, 'I am guilty in the sight of man but not of God.' Three 'medical gentlemen' had been asked to observe Frost while he was in prison and presented their findings to the court, which they did, stating that Frost 'was labouring under a moral or homicidal mania by which he was induced to believe that the dreadful act in question was praiseworthy and not a crime.' The jury returned a verdict of 'not guilty on account of insanity.' Frost was ordered to be confined in the Criminal Lunatic Asylum at St George's Fields, London, 'to await Her Majesty's pleasure.'

'Subject to Delusions'

William Howard was a hard man; he had been in the workhouse on seventy occasions and was brought before the magistrates six times for violent conduct before he was admitted, again, to the Norwich Workhouse in 1859. Howard had been acting oddly and had raised some concern when he 'exhibited some aberration of intellect' when he refused food for a while. He had also attempted to hang himself in the water closet. Medical opinion was that he was not insane, but that he was 'subject to delusions.' On 28 October 1858, Howard was seething after he had been reproved for failing to pick his proper quantity of oakum. Peter Willsea, an officer in the service of the Norwich Board of Guardians, was clearing away the cups after breakfast when Howard suddenly took up a fire pan and struck him two violent blows; one on the right temple, the other on the back of the head. As he was about to deliver a third blow, Henry Gowing Mitchell – another workhouse officer – warded off the blow. Howard struck out at Mitchell, severely wounding his arm. Brought before the Norwich Assizes in April 1859, Howard rambled on about 'Norman's will,' that he had been put into prison by parties who wished to get rid of him, that he had received what he called 'a reprieve through the King's warrant', and that he had been mistreated by his gaolers, who had made attempts to hang him. The jury were convinced that Howard was of unsound mind and he was ordered to be kept in custody 'during Her Majesty's pleasure.'

Chapter Eight

Poaching

The End of Billy Moonlight

The image of the poacher in the nineteenth century can be a romantic one of men who 'walked by night' to take a few rabbits for the pot, but in reality the exchanges between poachers and game-keepers would often result in vicious fights and deadly exchanges of gunfire as the poachers attempted to avoid capture. One such exchange terminated the life of notorious Lopham poacher, William 'Toy' Rayner, known to many locals as 'Billy Moonlight' – a man who always said he would rather kill a keeper than be taken.

Rayner and another man named Walter Mallows had set out on the night of Saturday, 18 December 1880 to go poaching for pheasants on land belonging to Cecil Montgomerie Esq., of Garboldisham Manor. On that same fateful night, keepers Samuel Rice and his son William had been joined by Thomas Blizzard, who had been roped in to joining the pair in an unarmed night-watch on the estate to earn a few pennies

At about 10.15 p.m., the three keepers were patrolling along a trackway known locally as 'Lovers Lane' when they spotted Rayner and Mallows walking towards them along the same

Exchanges between gamekeepers and poachers could often be violent and even cost lives.

track, and dived into a ditch to lay in wait for them. When Rayner and Mallows got to where the keepers were hiding Samuel Rice issued the challenge, 'What are you doing here?' Rayner replied, 'I will let you know what I am after,' and with an oath he then said, 'I have something here for you,' and cocked his shotgun. Rice ran up and closed on Rayner so he would have had difficulty presenting the gun at him, and succeeded in lifting the barrel up with his arm. They then got into a scrimmage. As Rice engaged Rayner, his son closed on Mallows. Rayner had hold of his gun by the barrel and struck out with the butt, dealing the younger Rice a blow to the top of his head and, as he did so, the gun went off. Samuel Rice released his grip and Rayner stumbled off. Rice's son called to his father to help him with Mallows and between them they secured the man as Blizzard set off in pursuit of Rayner.

Norfolk Constabulary police station at East Harling, *c.* 1880. (Norfolk Constabulary Archive)

After about 100 yards, Rayner could run no more and collapsed to the ground; the shot had caught him and blood was pouring out of the wound. Samuel Rice ran to the Fox Inn at Garboldisham in order to get someone to summon a doctor for him and alert the police. Mallows was taken into custody by PC Reeve, and was later removed to Harling police station. Rayner was carried on a gate to the inn, where he was attended by Hopton surgeon Mr Edwin John Gurdon. The wound proved to be a mortal one and 'Billy Moonlight' died the following night.

The inquest was held at the Fox Inn, before H.E. Garrod Esq., Coroner for the Duke of Norfolk's Liberty. Surgeon Gurdon testified the shot was consistent with the story told by the keepers; the Coroner and jury were satisfied and a verdict of 'accidental death from gunshot wound' was recorded.

'Owley' Lemmon

John Lemmon was a poacher and ne're-do-well in the Shotesham area during the 1860s. He had managed to get away with many things, but his actions on Saturday, 28 November 1863 got him into serious trouble for the first time. Two under-keepers named Watson and Garrod were keeping night watch on the estate of Mr Fellowes

The Shotesham gamekeepers and brushers in the early twentieth century.

of Shotesham, when they heard three gunshots fired on a portion of the land known as 'Low Shotesham Wood.' Watson and Garrod went to alert the Head Keeper, Mr Charles Long. Long and Watson set off towards where the gunshots had been heard, leaving Garrod behind to keep watch. Long and Watson proceeded along a lane where they saw two men walking away from the wood with guns in their hands. When the two men were about thirty yards off, both keepers recognised one of the men as 'Owley' Lemmon before the poachers ran off. Watson and Long gave chase. The unrecognised poacher made good use of his legs and disappeared, but the keepers closed in on Owley and when they were about six yards from him he turned, pulled his gun out from under his coat and cried out, 'Damn your hearts, if you don't keep back I'll shoot you.' The words had hardly left his lips when he levelled his gun at Long and discharged the shotgun. Fortunately, Owley's only shot hit his legs, and, as he was stoutly dressed, the shot did not cause him too severe an injury.

Owley then walked backwards, brandishing his stick at Watson, threatening that he would re-load and shoot again. Watson then rushed at him and received a violent blow from the stock of Owley's gun, which broke the weapon. He then pulled a stone out of his pocket and threw it at Long before making his escape.

The problem for Owley was that he was a local reprobate poaching on local land. Long knew Owley Lemmon only too well and when he informed the police of what had happened, a warrant was issued for his arrest. Lemmon had been seen in the area on the night and during the following morning, but when the police came for him there was no sign of Owley.

Lemmon's description was circulated and he was eventually tracked down by PC Wilson on 5 December, when he was found on board a steamer about to leave Great Yarmouth for London. He came quietly and when brought before the assizes, his defence argued that he had an alibi and had been drinking at Mr Nicholls's on Ber Street in Norwich on the night in question. The jury were not convinced and Lemmon was found guilty of unlawful wounding and sent down for eighteen months. Owley continued his life of crime when he came out, with more petty thieving and poaching, until he was caught horse stealing. After due trial at the Norfolk Assizes in June 1869, his previous convictions counted against him and Owley was imprisoned for seven years.

The Most Notorious Poacher

Fred Rolfe was proclaimed the 'King of the Norfolk Poachers' in *I Walked by Night* (1935), but the most infamous of all the Norfolk poachers was Robert Henry Large. Born in Great Witchingham in 1867, the eighth of ten children from the good family of John Large, a local butcher, and his wife Elizabeth, Robert grew up in Hackford but was a wayward lad from an early age. Then, in maturity, he gained a formidable reputation, not only as a poacher but as an escaper from the clutches of the law. In December 1887, he was arrested for an assault upon a constable at Great Witchingham and put into Reepham Bridewell, from which he escaped a couple of days later and was not recaptured until January 1888, when he was traced to a house in North Heigham. Tried and found guilty for the assault, he was removed to HM Prison Norwich. Like all prisoners he was set to work; on Saturday 11 February he was employed in the prison yard which was surrounded by a wall of some considerable height, but shortly before noon he was missing and the ensuing search for him revealed that, by some means, he and another prisoner named George Annison had managed to escape; Large and Annison became the first prisoners to escape from the new prison, which had only been opened a few months earlier.

While on the run, Large taunted the prison authorities by returning his prison-issue trousers to HM Prison Norwich by parcel post, with a small covering note stating: 'With Thanks – Robert Large.' Annison was not keen on life on the run and knew he would be inviting recapture by returning to his home at Martham, however, the following afternoon Large was traced to his father's house at Lenwade. At 4 p.m. the county police team, lead by Superintendent Grimes, with Inspector Palmer and constables Southgate, Allen and Rix made their bid to capture Large. PC Southgate entered the house by the back door, leaving PC Allen to guard that exit while PC Rix stood at the front door. Southgate went up one flight of stairs and heard a movement in a room, which he entered just in time to see Large going out of the house by another flight of stairs. Leaping across the room, Southgate saw Large at the foot of the stairs and at once 'took a header' down and landed near Large, who he pinned down with one arm and shouted for the other officers. Large turned, thinking he had only one man to deal with and threatened to fight for his liberty but before he could make good his threat, PC Rix was there to help restrain him, quickly followed by the other officers. Large struggled violently but was soon handcuffed and led away to Lenwade railway station, swearing he would wreak his vengeance on the officers.

Large's exploits over the years had given him a bit of a folk hero identity in the countryside and the news that Large had been apprehended at his father's house spread like wildfire. So, as they approached the station, a large crowd had already gathered, cheering for Large and hissing at and hustling the police officers. News soon spread to Norwich and the train carrying Large to Norwich City station was met there by a large crowd of sympathisers and friends of Large. It was with some difficulty that the police made their way through the crowd and bundled Large into a cab. This vehicle was soon surrounded by 'roughs', who attempted to overturn it and set Large free, but fortunately the driver whipped up the horse and managed to drive off and Large was returned to prison.

After having served his prison time Large was soon back to his old tricks. On the night of 17 January 1889, Robert Large and one of his cronies named John Smith were out poaching in Edgefield, when they were challenged by Robert Middleton as they came out of his garden at about 10 p.m. Smith replied by saying to Large, 'This fellow says someone has been in his garden.' Large immediately replied to Middleton, 'If you say I've been into your garden I'll give you something.' Middleton replied that he had not said he had been into the garden, but hardly had he got those words out when Large rushed at him and knocked him down with a tremendous blow on the head. Middleton managed to pull himself up and made towards his cottage. Large said, 'It's no use running, you can't get away.' Large was soon upon him again and knocked him through a fence into a pool of water. Middleton struggled out and started to run towards the house of neighbour, Mr Etchells the schoolmaster, but Large caught him and dealt him another blow to the top of the head, flooring him. The poor man was then threatened that if he did not get up, Large would kick him up; in saying so, he put the boot in and when Middleton got to his feet, both Smith and Large set about him and punched him to the ground. Once more he struggled to his feet; Large then slung his arm around Middleton's neck, got him into a headlock and punched his face mercilessly. Middleton was beat so badly he went in and out of consciousness but managed to say, 'I pray God save you from such practices as these.' Middleton was then kicked in the chest again, but managed to struggle away and got into Mr Etchells' house.

Mr Hales the surgeon attended to Middleton, he knew the man well but when he saw him after the assault he could not recognise him. A wound above his left ear bled for days after, the injuries to his chest caused difficulty to his breathing; indeed, it was uncertain if Middleton would recover from his attack until several days after. Large was a wanted man; a number of warrants from both the Norwich City and County Police had been issued for his arrest for a number of incidents but, as ever, he proved to be a very elusive man.

On Friday, 1 March 1889, the County Police received intelligence that Large and one of his known accomplices, Smith, may be found drinking in the Little John public house on Northumberland Street.

Inspector Rix, Sergeant Chambers and PC's Flint, Sent and Lynn of Norfolk Constabulary proceeded to the tavern, and at about 9.30 p.m. spotted Smith and Large, who were enjoying themselves in the bar. Sergeant Chambers approached them and informed them of the reason for their meeting. Large and Smith expressed their surprise but before they could give any answer Chambers seized Large, who, true to form, resisted capture with all his strength; despite twisting, turning, writhing and wrestling, he failed to free himself from the grip of the stalwart officer. Others in the pub were not above attempts to hinder the arrest but Chambers got the cuffs on Large. Large then went into a fury, smashing windows near him, kicking in the panel of the door and contriving to drag Chambers into the street. More people gathered there and hustled around the Police Sergeant and, in a moment, Large was able to rip free from him, smash the cuffs that held him and run off down the street. PC Lynn had come to the aid of Chambers but he had been unable to reach him, owing to the hostile crowd. However, as Large made off, Lynn followed in pursuit with Chambers and they managed to get hold of Large again, but he was not coming quietly and delivered a vicious kick to Lynn in the ribs. Struggle on they did and another set of 'darbies' were soon restraining Large. They returned to the pub, where Smith came far more quietly, and then both Large and Smith were removed to custody.

The 'darbies', as used in the arrest of Robert Large.

NORWICH CITY POLICE.

Photo and description of

ROBERT LARGE,

alias "Seymour," an ex-convict and notorious poacher, wanted on warrant in this City, charged with assault on Police on 13th August, 1904.

Aged 37 years, height 6 feet 1 inch, swarthy complexion, dark brown hair, brown moustache, brown eyes, peppermints build, stoops slightly, long, swinging gait; a native of Co. Winchingham, Norfolk, Marks:—scar middle forehead, left side neck, scar bone left thumb, palm of hand, back little finger, top joint left little finger contracted, scar inside and a outside front right wrist, scar right of back and front left shin, mole left shoulder.

Dressed usually in light brown coat and vest, cord trousers, cap, and heavy face boots.

May be found associating with poachers and thieves, or at low Public-houses.

Please cause every possible enquiry to be made for this man, and if found, arrest and wire me, when an officer shall be sent for him, or any information obtained kindly communicate to

E. F. WINCH.

Norwich City Police's wanted poster for Robert Large, 1904. (Norfolk Constabulary Archive)

On Monday, 22 July 1889, John Smith and Robert Large, both aged twenty-two, were brought before the Norfolk Assizes, charged with 'feloniously, unlawfully and maliciously wounding Robert Middleton with intent to do him grievous bodily harm.' The notoriety of Large drew a crowd that packed out the courthouse; both prisoners were attended by a pair of burly prison warders in the dock. Smith pleaded not guilty, but Large, who was recorded as presenting 'a very untidy appearance and most morose countenance', refused to plead or answer to the charge. The trial was brief and after a retirement of just three minutes, the jury returned to announce that both men were found guilty. The judge did not hold back his opinions when passing sentence, describing the offence as 'of the most ruffianly character and a disgrace to a civilized county,' and went on to say, 'if such offences come before me they come before the wrong Judge to be let off lightly.' Smith was given five years and left the dock smiling, even taking time to wave at the gallery. Large was handed down ten years penal servitude. He received his sentence in silence and was removed from the dock by the warders.

Large served his sentence at HM Prison Rochester but on his return to Norfolk, after his release, he got himself into trouble again when he assaulted a police officer in 1904. Determined to make a new start, Large headed for somewhere nobody knew him, at Goole in Yorkshire, where he worked as a coal trimmer on the docks under the alias of George Seymour, where he was remembered as 'a well-spoken and educated' man who obtained the nickname of 'Gentleman George'. Large married Lily Bunting under his own name, settled down, raised a family, and lived the rest of his life quietly until his death in 1949.

The Notorious 'Shirts' Rudd

Charles 'Shirts' Rudd and Walter Wylie were a pair of Norfolk poachers who had 'walked by night' for many years and had acquired not only notoriety but a certain 'local hero' status.

On the night of 27 December 1895, Rudd and Wylie were out poaching on Lord Hasting's estate at Briston when they were challenged by the gamekeeper John Fish and two of his under-keepers, John Cubitt and William Eke. The keepers only had sticks with them but that was no cause for mercy from Rudd and Wylie, who immediately levelled and discharged both their guns at the keepers. Eke was shot in the shoulder and Cubitt took some of the shot to his head. The brave keepers still managed to secure Wylie but Rudd would not be such an easy catch. He swung at Fish with his gun, causing a nasty wound to his right temple. Although somewhat stunned by this, Fish closed on Rudd and overcame him but the poacher managed to make his escape and ran off into the darkness.

The keepers were determined Rudd was not going to get away and informed the police. Inspector Willmott of Holt police was soon on the case with seven of his men, and, assisted by Superintendent Grimes and three officers from Aylsham district, they formed a 'task force' to track down Rudd.

The problem was that Rudd was a local character, even something of a hero to some, and had many friends across the area only too willing to hide him away and put the officers of the law off his trail. After a week of pursuit the reward of £10, which had been offered for information of Rudd's whereabouts, loosened lips and the police team narrowed their search to Edgefield. The constables were paired with some of Lord Hasting's keepers and surrounded the village, closing in on Thurning Barn Plantation. Rudd's mother lived nearby in the hamlet of Crymer's Beck, near Briston, so a smaller party of officers were sent there to interview her. She claimed she had not seen her son for some time, nor did she know his whereabouts, but then a three-pint jug was spotted by a small barrow shed in her back garden. On closer examination it was found to be filled with steaming hot tea. This had hardly been discovered before Rudd could see the game was up and bolted. Police whistles were blown and police and gamekeepers came running from all directions. Rudd was eventually run to ground on Briston Common while running for Thurning Mill.

Handcuffed and loaded into a cart with a number of police officers escorting him to Holt lock-up, Rudd remarked, 'Give my compliments to Lord Hastings and tell him I shall have some more of his pheasants when I come out. I suppose I shall get five years for this job.'

Wylie and Rudd were brought before Mr Justice Willis at the Norfolk Assizes, charged with feloniously wounding John Fish and on an indictment of feloniously wounding under-keepers Cubitt and Eke, with intent to murder them. Found guilty on all counts, Wylie received three years penal servitude whereas Rudd, having been convicted on several previous occasions, was sent down for seven years.

It was not long before 'Shirts' was in trouble again. According to evidence given at a special sessions held at Holt in May 1905, Rudd was out on the road in Edgefield with another man named 'Jumbo' Warner, where they were spotted looking in the hedgerows on either side of the road by PC Moore of Baconsthorpe. PC Moore challenged Rudd, believing he had unlawfully obtained eggs about his person and proceeded to search him. Rudd flew in a rage and threatened to knock the constable's brains out and punched him in the mouth. Both men began to grapple and fell to the floor, where Moore attempted to handcuff Rudd. Warner then waded in, thumping Moore on the head. Moore tried to stand up but was immediately knocked down again and rendered unconscious by Rudd. As his senses returned to him, he found Rudd standing over him with a large stick in his hand saying, 'I have a good mind to finish you now. I shall get six years for it.' He then called to Warner, 'You're not afraid, are you Jack?' To which Warner replied, 'It would take more than that to frighten me.' Rudd then went over to Warner and suggested, 'Let's finish the b****** off.' PC Moore managed to get himself to Chapman's farm and from there was removed to Holt, where he was treated by Dr Hales. Rudd and Warner were tracked down and brought before the Norfolk Assizes, where they were sent down again.

Chapter Nine

Smugglers

King of the Norfolk Smugglers

Smuggling had been known along the Norfolk coast for centuries but was at its height during the eighteenth and early nineteenth centuries, as Daniel Defoe commented in *A Tour Thro' the Whole Island of Great Britain* (1724):

> From Clye, we go to Masham, and to Wells, all towns on the coast, in each whereof there is a very considerable Trade carried on with Holland for Corn, which that Part of the country is very full of: I say nothing of the Great Trade driven here from Holland, back again to England, because I take it to be Trade carried on with much less Honesty than Advantage; especially while the clandestine trade or the art of smuggling was so much in practice.

For many on the periphery, smuggling was just another part of country life, a bit of excitement by moonlight helping get the cargoes of luxury goods such as brandy, Geneva gin, tea, tobacco and lace ashore, or running them inland. The pay was good too; helping the smugglers, one labouring man could earn the same in one night as he could for a week's labour on a farm. It would also be a chance to acquire a few treats for yourself and in doing so, all concerned could also have the personal satisfaction of 'giving one in the eye' to the hated excise.

But if you pried or became tempted to cross or inform on the smugglers you would leave yourself open to deadly reprisals. Tales were well known of informers being dragged from their bed in the dead of night by bands of angry smugglers, beaten and whipped in the street and then being dragged off, never to be seen again.

The authorities knew the smugglers ensured that locals remained tight-lipped but they would offer some serious rewards in an attempt to loosen them, for instance, the following handbill was published in 1768:

> A large body of smugglers, having murdered Peter Haslip, tide-surveyor of Yarmouth port, and dangerously wounded several others, who had seized a large quantity of excisable goods, which the said smugglers rescued and carried off with them; His Majesty's Pardon, as usual, is offered for taking the offenders and the Commissioners of Excise promise a reward of One Hundred Pounds for taking any of them.

Smugglers, and their associates, were not able to go about their business unimpeded; the excise was often backed up by local regular mounted troops and yeomanry patrolling the coastal roads and tracks, while the revenue cutter patrolled the sea lanes, but

Smugglers unloading their contraband onto the beach.

even the millers were 'in on it' and upon sight of the revenue boat would drop their sails to warn the smugglers of its approach, occasionally there would be no warning and the smugglers would be caught in the act, but they seldom came quietly.

In one case, recorded in January 1822, a smuggling boat landed eighty tubs of gin and brandy on the secluded beach at Snettisham. The excise men were close by and seized the cargo but a crowd of about 100 people appeared out of the gloom, armed with 'bludgeons and fowling pieces' and assisted the smugglers to retrieve some of their confiscated goods and allowed the smugglers to make good on their escape in their boat, while those on the beach made their getaway on the twenty or thirty horses and carts that they had waiting on the beach to receive the contraband.

The revenue men did have their successes. In the winter of 1812/13, a smuggling cutter with some 600 casks of Geneva gin on board was captured off Salthouse by the Sheringham revenue boat. The vessel was taken to Blakeney harbour and the cargo deposited in the King's warehouse at Cley. In December 1824, Customs officers seized 120 half-ankers of Geneva gin, nineteen bags of tobacco, ten bags of snuff, ten boxes of cigars and two Chinese ornaments on the beach and lodged the goods in the Cley Custom House. After 'a desperate affray' on 26 February 1833, Lieutenant George Howes RN, of the Weybourne Preventative Station, and a party of coastguards under his command, surprised a large number of smugglers at Cley. The smugglers put up a fearsome resistance and the coastguards were caused to discharge their weapons several

Smugglers loading their goods onto ponies ready for the 'run' inland.

times in self-defence. The haul they seized was, however, impressive; 127 half ankers of brandy and 3-4,000 pounds of manufactured tobacco. Not all the revenue men were whiter than white either, many were tempted, some were caught, among them William Howes, an officer of the Customs, and Cook Flowers, an excise officer, who were found guilty at the Norfolk Assizes in August 1807, of stealing a quantity of prize brandy from a Great Yarmouth storehouse, over which they had been put in charge. Both received a sentence of transportation for seven years.

If a smuggler or one of their associates was captured, the problem faced by the prosecutors was getting the case against them to stick, as most people outside the revenue and the law would simply refuse to testify against them. Many smugglers had also acquired some powerful allies. For instance, Joseph Wake, with four others, had been tried at the Norfolk Assizes for assaulting James Mackarel, an Officer of the Revenue, whilst in the execution of his duty at North Walsham in February 1805. Mackarel had seized a number of smuggled spirits that had been condemned and ordered to be sold by public auction on a market day. A crowd assembled, among the leaders of which were the five defendants, who had managed to get into the place of sale and hustled Mackarel, and, in the confusion, saw the opportunity to hack at his ankles with their boots. The injuries he suffered left Mackarel lame for several weeks after.

At the trial, Wake swore he had been selling wheat in the market when the mob arose, carrying him along with them, and that he could not extricate himself from the crowd. He adamantly stated that he had no intention of interrupting Mackarel. An affidavit from the Clerk of the Corn Market corroborated Wake's statement. It is also intriguing to note a number of the leading gentlemen of the county, including Horatio, Lord Walpole, Charles Windham Esq. and Sir Roger Kerrison, Bart., sent favourable statements of Wake's good character. It does make one wonder how a lowly corn seller could have got to know such men, but then the gentry were often good customers of the smugglers...

Things had changed little since the 1780s, when notorious smuggling captain, William Kemble and his crew ran goods from Dunkirk to the Norfolk shore aboard their ship the *Lively*.

The gravestone marking the grave of Dragoon William Webb in the churchyard at Old Hunstanton. It states:
In memory of William Webb, late of the 15th D'ns, who was shot from his Horse by a party of Smugglers on the 26 of Sept. 1784.
I am not dead but sleepeth here,
And when the Trumpet Sound I will appear
Four balls thro' me Pearced there way:
Hard it was. I'd no time to pray
This stone that here you Do see
My Comerades Erected for the sake of me.'

Kemble, a son of King's Lynn, had built a formidable smuggling network along the coast and deep into the county. He had a few scrapes with the law but had managed to evade detection and capture on numerous occasions – that was until September 1784. Excise officers had seized a large quantity of Kemble's contraband and chased him and his crew off Thornham beach on the night of 24 September. The following day, Kemble kept the *Lively* hovering off the coast and attempted to discharge the rest of his cargo at Old Hunstanton in the early hours of 26 September, but was chased off again, with the loss of more of his contraband. Kemble saw red and wildly resolved to take it back by force.

Kemble landed with an armed party and was told by one of his village contacts that the seized goods had been taken to Clare's farmhouse and were under the guard of two excise men and five dragoons. Aware that a further party from the 15th Light Dragoons and mounted excise officers were approaching, Kemble spread his men along the field side of the hedgerow along the lane, with their weapons facing into the lane. The party of dragoons were well lit in the moonlight and suspected nothing as they rode into the ambush.

Dragoon William Webb (aged twenty-six) was first to fall in the hail of lead from the smugglers' long-arms; others suffered

A short distance from Webb's grave is that of William Green, who died the following day of the wounds he received in the same ambush: 'Here lie the mangled remains of poor William Green, an Honest Officer of the Government, who in the faithful discharge of his duty was inhumanely murdered by a gang of Smugglers in this Parish, September 27th, 1784.'

severe injuries, among them Excise Officer William Green (thirty-seven), who fell mortally wounded and died the following day. Kemble and two of his men, Henry Gunton and Thomas Williams, were captured and held in Norwich Castle to await trial and were brought under armed escort to Thetford for the Norfolk Assizes, in March 1785. Williams turned King's Evidence and the case against Kemble and Gunton was well proven in court but, to the great surprise of many concerned, the jury found Gunton and Kemble not guilty.

Mr Murphy, the counsel for the prosecution, could not disguise his disgust and stated:

[…] if a Norfolk jury was determined not to find these men guilty of these atrocious crimes on the grounds they were smugglers and had the sympathy of the people it was an end to all justice.

He moved for, and was granted, a retrial under a fresh indictment with a new jury. This jury heard the case then retired for three hours for their deliberations, but still returned a verdict of 'not guilty.' With the failure of the trial prosecutions, Kemble and Gunton were brought before the Court of Exchequer at Westminster, charged with bringing ashore goods and failing to pay import duty, before being ordered to pay £303. The court was adjourned and the smugglers were granted bail. Needless to say, they walked out of the court and jumped bail.

Smugglers and their contraband; once a regular feature of life in the coastal areas of Norfolk.

Two months after Kemble's trial, a hardened petty criminal named Peter Bullard, who had been involved with Kemble's gang of smugglers, was arrested for stealing a brown mare from Martin Greenacre at Ingoldisthorpe. Tried at the 1785 Norfolk Summer Assizes, he was found guilty and sentenced to death. While lodged in the condemned cell Bullard dictated his confession, in which he stated:

> I cannot help mentioning the unhappy circumstance which happened at Hunstanton when Webb the soldier and Mr Green the excise-officer lost their lives; for though I was not guilty of the act of murder, still I consider myself as accessory for being concerned with Kemble the smuggler and his crew, as I was assisting in unloading the vessel and carrying off the run goods; and not withstanding their being acquitted by the jury, whose consciences must answer for the act and whose names have been published by order of the Lord Lieutenant. I do declare that I saw Kemble fire the first gun and the soldier fall and then with threats heard him compel his men to fire, when Mr Green received his mortal wound.

Bullard signed his confession with his mark, an 'x'. He freely admitted to his crimes, agreed with the justness of the punishment and went contritely to the gallows on Castle Hill on 6 August 1785. Kemble, however, went back to his old ways and carried on his smuggling activities for many a year.

Chapter Ten

Thieves

'I'll make the old woman a liar!'

Mary Taylor was an attractive young servant girl employed by Mrs Ann Wright, the landlady of the Queen's Head on the High Street at King's Lynn, in 1731. Mary worked hard at her job and turned quite a few heads; so it came as quite a surprise and disappointment when she started walking out with George Smith. Smith was a ne'er-do-well character and was well known across the port of Lynn as a rogue and petty thief, but apart from the odd exchange with members of the 'The Watch' (the forerunner of the police) he had escaped the clutches of the law. He was also one of those rugged types who had a certain appeal and reputation with the impressionable girls of the servant class in the town. Most of the criminal fraternity of Lynn simply gave him a wide berth, not just for fear of his volatile temper but for the schemes he dreamt up, and in which he wished to inveigle others, which were often far-fetched and could result with any captured culprits dangling on the end of the hangman's rope.

Mary Taylor soon became infatuated with Smith and he soon saw that he could manipulate her to become his accomplice in a robbery at the premises of her employer. Smith assured Mary that she would not have to commit the robbery herself; all she had to do was wait until all had gone to bed and then, in the darkest of the chime hours, he would hide himself near the back door and wait for it to be opened by Mary. She could then creep back to bed, Smith would do his dirty work, and then she could pretend to awake with the rest of the household and be shocked by the crime that had been committed while they were all, allegedly, asleep. Compared to his other harebrained schemes, this one was simplicity itself.

Mary waited until all was still in the house; the pub had cleared out long ago and she silently felt her way downstairs. She then made her way to the door, placed her hand on the freezing cold handle of the large throw bolt on the door and slid it back. Slowly, she opened the door and the bright moonlight flooded in as it swung open. Her heart was in her throat as her lover emerged from the shadows and she felt a little frisson for the danger and excitement of the event. Smith pushed past the girl with little acknowledgement of her being there – he was set on finding the money – and started to fumble his way around. The moonlight helped him get some of his bearings but the darkness held a minefield of noisy pewter pots, plates and mugs that made quite a clatter as he blundered his way around the darker recesses of the pub. Some accounts state that young Mary was on her way back to her room when she encountered the landlady, Mrs Wright, coming down the stairs as she was going up. Curious as to what Mary was doing and still hearing the noises downstairs, Mrs Wright pushed the girl aside and ran down the stairs with her lamp and issued the challenge 'Who's there?'

Smith was thrown into a panic; his exit was blocked and he was cornered. His typical rage and no doubt some blind panic overtook him and he hurled himself at Mrs Wright. She was, however, a pretty feisty woman and was not going to be defeated so easily and she fought back furiously and began screaming. Smith lunged at the poor woman, his hand wrapping around her throat, throttling the life out of her. When she was still and the red mist in front of his eyes had cleared, Smith sensed that the woman's cries had alerted the neighbours and made a break for it, but he was

King's Lynn Guildhall Courthouse and Town Gaol (right), *c.* 1910.

soon brought into custody and thrown into the cells of the Gaol House.

Smith thought he may mitigate his case by implicating others. After a number of allegations naming other male accomplices he threw in the name of his sweetheart, Mary Taylor. It was quite probable that neither of them could have quite foreseen where this twist of fate could lead. The crime of opening a locked door for a criminal struck at the very heart of the sacred trust between servant and master, or mistress. At a time when every household would still work along the hierarchical lines; every household being a microcosm of the state with head of the house as King, mistress as Queen and servants as minions, the crime committed by Mary was considered Petty Treason and was punishable by burning at the stake.

George Smith was found guilty of murder and poor Mary Taylor was found guilty of Petty Treason. Both were carted to Lynn's Tuesday market place. A massive crowd lined the route to jeer at Smith and show pity for Taylor. Smith was first to his death and, as he mounted the gallows, he sneered at the crowd. As the executioner adjusted the rope around his neck Smith kicked off his shoes, exclaiming, 'My mother always told me I should die in my shoes. There! Just for jolly, I'll make the old woman a liar!' As Smith kicked his last on the rope, just seventeen yards away they

A horrific end as a woman is burned at the stake.

lit the bundles of faggots beneath Mary Taylor and sent her to her doom, consumed by fire at the stake.

Grand Larceny at Norwich

Following a number of robberies that had occurred in Norwich over the previous twelve months, two likely culprits were brought before the Norfolk Assizes in August 1804. Father and son, Benjamin and John Pritchard (alias Price) were indicted with 'grand larceny' on 17 August 1804, for breaking into the counting-house of Messrs Gurney and Bland in St Saviour's, Norwich, and stealing several bank notes and cash to the value of £120.

Testimony was given by Edmund Sparshall, clerk to Gurney and Bland, who stated he had left the counting house on the evening in question at 5.30p.m., leaving cash and notes in the drawer of an iron safe. The notes were in a bag, folded up and covered with a piece of brown paper. He then locked the safe and went away with the key in his pocket. The following day he found the lock rather stiff when he unlocked the safe. Once he had opened the safe, he saw the brown paper but, to his horror, the bag containing the money was gone. When Sparshall took out the key he also noted that it was covered in wax.

Suspicions fell on John Pritchard and the Mayor's Constable, Robert Paraman, went with two other constables named Cordran and Church to John Prichard's house the following day, armed with a search warrant. When they knocked, John Pritchard came to the door and gave no objection to the search. In the house they also found Pritchard's father, Benjamin, and a Mr Mendham, the Norwich Expedition coachman. Mr Pritchard senior appeared very uncomfortable and attempted to leave, but the constables prevented him and asked where he lived. Pritchard denied that he lived in Norwich and claimed he had slept the previous night at the Black Horse in Tombland. Further enquiries revealed Mr Pritchard did in fact occupy a house in St Paul's, Norwich, and when the constables undertook a search they discovered an earthenware bread pot covered with a greasy knife cloth; inside were five £5 notes from Messrs Gurney, a £2 note and five £1 Bank of England notes. Under the stairs, Constable Cordran also discovered two bags of picklock and skeleton keys, as well as a number of others filled up with wax. Among these were two keys which were proved to be able to open the outer and inner doors of the counting house. When questioned about how they came to be found in his possession, Pritchard claimed they had been 'thrown over the garden wall.'

At the trial, John Pritchard called witnesses who vouched for him and confirmed that he carried on the trade of a watchmaker and appeared to be 'of good character'. Like so many trials in the nineteenth century, much of the evidence was circumstantial and Mr Justice Heath observed, 'There is no positive proof of the prisoners' having committed the offence with which they are charged.' However, he did agree the strongest evidence was against the father. The jury retired for about ten minutes and returned with the verdict, finding Benjamin Pritchard 'guilty' and acquitting his son. In passing sentence the judge pointed out to Pritchard that had his offence amounted to burglary, he should have certainly have left him for execution; as it was not burglary, he adjudged him to be transported for seven years. Benjamin Pritchard was fifty-five years old when he was taken aboard the prison hulk *Laurel* at Portsmouth, in a delivery of convicts on 10 March 1805. He was released in 1811, after serving his time.

Was John Pritchard tarred with the same brush because of the wrongs of his father? Either way he was no angel, for after his first trial he was brought up on a second indictment of presenting a loaded pistol at a constable named Christmas Church. The incident occurred after a neighbour of Pritchard, named William Wilde, had seen him leaving his house at odd hours and behaving in a suspicious manner on a number of occasions. As a number of burglaries were being committed in the city at the time, he communicated his suspicions about Pritchard to the Mayor, and Constables Church and Cordran were ordered to keep a watch on him on the following night. They saw him come out of his house and waited until his return some time later. Church stepped out from the shadows and seized Pritchard, who immediately presented a pistol at him and cocked it. It was a vicious looking firearm with two rifle barrels and a spring bayonet. The constables managed to disarm Pritchard and searched him. About his person they found another pistol, a box of phosphorus with matches, a pair of muffles for his feet and eleven picklock keys. The pistol Pritchard had aimed at Constable Church was found to be loaded. The downfall of this case, however, was the letter of the law. Pritchard had been charged with presenting and attempting to fire the pistol at Constable Church and, despite being seen to unbar and cock said pistol, Mr Justice Heath was of the opinion it was more necessary to prove Pritchard had pulled the trigger – which had not been done in the evidence presented at the trial – therefore, he felt he had no other option than to direct the jury to acquit Pritchard. Jane Pritchard, who had been due to appear for an assault upon the constable who had apprehended her brother, was also acquitted after no evidence was called against her.

The Beast of Hindringham

Robert Bushell was born in Hindringham on 14 November 1835, the youngest of six children of James and Susanna Bushell. His father eked out a meagre living as a horse hair weaver and died at the Horsham St Faith's Workhouse in March 1850. Robert had always been a bit of a handful and after the death of his father he took to petty crime, making his first appearance at the Norfolk Quarter Sessions in June 1852, where he was convicted of larceny and sentenced to one calendar month in Castle Gaol. He was brought before the Lent Assizes in March 1853, where he was convicted of felony and was imprisoned for three months. In January 1858, he was back in court on another charge of larceny and was found guilty and, in light of his previous convictions, was this time sent down for three years. It seems that while inside he did not learn the lesson in punishment intended for him, but learned more skills of how to go about his nefarious acts without being caught. However, like so many who commit crimes of a serious nature, it was a minor offence that brought him to justice again. In the case of Bushell it was a coat, valued at 10 shillings, which was the property of Samuel Money of Hindringham. On the same day, Bushell also stole a shirt, a pinafore and a cloth from George Cooper, another Hindringham resident. Bushell pleaded guilty at the Norfolk Quarter Sessions in January 1867 and was sent down for twelve months.

Bushell left prison more embittered than ever and in November 1868 he vented his spleen when he broke into the Fakenham Toll-Gate House. Inside he found the occupants, Lydia Large and Anne Lake. Bushell viciously beat and assaulted both women, dragging one of them by the heels up the road so that she was exposed indecently. Indeed, newspaper reports stated that 'his treatment [of the women] was that of a wild beast.' When Bushell was brought before the Norfolk Assizes in March 1869, the press described him as 'a villainous looking character' and that he did not appear to be too concerned about his situation – Bushell had become a hardened criminal. He was found guilty, but, before passing sentence, the judge was moved to comment on Bushell's attack of the two women, stating that, in his view, 'more cruel

The outrage at the Fakenham Toll-Gate House, 1868.

treatment inflicted could hardly be imagined.' When his Lordship asked Bushell if he had any previous convictions, he replied, 'Yes; that's right enough.' Bushell was sentenced to ten years, most of which he spent at Portland Convict Prison.

The Pursuit of Henry Hindle

On the evening of Thursday, 21 August 1862, the shop of working jeweller Mr Mills, on Old Jetty Road, Great Yarmouth, was subjected to a robbery. Mills lived on the premises and was out at the time, but his wife and daughter were in the room immediately behind the shop between 8 p.m. and 8.30 p.m., when the thieves extracted nine or ten gold and silver watches that normally hung on hooks in the shop window. This they managed to do without attracting the attention of the family within. Around 8.30 p.m., Mr Mills returned to his shop and immediately noticed the missing property from the window and set off directly to the police station; Detective Sergeant Berry was instantly despatched to discover the perpetrators. Berry knew Yarmouth well (he had a few informers) and was soon told of some 'well-known characters' who had been seen in the neighbourhood. After receiving some information, Berry was soon on his way to one of the known haunts of one of the suspects, the lodgings of Henry Hindle, who lived with Emma Richmond – another local thief of some notoriety. On knocking at the door and enquiring for Hindle, Berry was informed by Richmond that he was not there. Berry said he intended to wait until he returned and as he did so, expressed a wish to search the house.

No objection was raised and Berry began his search. He found nothing until he reached up a chimney in an upper room, where, in a hole in the brickwork, his hand fell upon some old rags. Fixing his fingers around them, the detective brought them out and, feeling something in their folds, carefully unwrapped them to reveal a gold and a silver lever watch. Sensing he was on the right track, Berry placed Richmond in the charge of another officer and went off in search of another gang member named Samuel Elvin. Berry found Elvin in a low public house known as the Princess Charlotte, where he was preparing for bed. After securing Elvin, Berry paid a visit to Charlotte Street, where he arrested William Newson on suspicion of being another member of the gang of thieves, but Hindle, the man suspected of being the gang leader, could not be found. Berry's attention was, however, drawn by the suspicious behaviour of a man named Cockerel, who appeared to be watching Berry's movements.

Before giving up his search for the night, the gallant detective and one of his colleagues visited Cockerel's house (one of 'indifferent repute'), in an area of the town known as The Conge, shortly before 1 a.m. on Friday. Knocking on the door garnered no reply, but their enquiries as to the whereabouts of Cockerel received a response from within. The lady inside stated that he was out and because of that, she could not admit the police. The situation was not pleasing to Berry and just as he and his colleague were considering busting the door down, it was opened to them. On entering an upper room in the lodgings, they found

Cockerel, who indignantly demanded what their business was. Berry stated that he had come to search the house and continued to do so, but found nothing. That was until he noticed a slight fall of soot in one of the grates and, turning his lantern up the chimney, found none other than Henry Hindle hiding up there! Berry called upon him to come down and surrender, but Hindle only pushed himself further up the chimney. Thinking it might be a way of hastening his descent, some shavings and brown paper were lit in the grate, but this only caused Hindle to work his way yet further up the chimney.

A typical Great Yarmouth row, c. 1900.

However, his ascent was blocked by the narrowing of the chimney but, undaunted, he broke a hole through the chimney into an attic. Berry punched a hole in the ceiling at once and succeeded in grasping Hindle's leg, but was caused to release his hold when Hindle dealt him a blow from a poker, which he had somehow managed to find in the small space.

Hindle was trapped in the attic so he returned to the chimney and used the poker to lever away tiles and made his way onto the roof of the house, on which (without boots it was noted) 'he ran about with the agility of a cat.' Ladders were obtained by the police, and Berry, supported by a formidable staff of police and people attracted to the spot, was soon in hot pursuit, but was hindered by Hindle tearing off the tiles, slates or anything else he could move from the roof tops he ran across, and hurling them at his pursuers. Hindle kept the officers of the law at bay for more than four hours, during which time he kept up a constant shower of missiles – one of which struck PC Brown, cutting his head badly.

Favoured by daylight, the police slowly drove Hindle back and, just as it appeared as though he had no means of escape, he leapt from one roof to a lower roof across an alley, a distance of some 15ft, but when he landed on the other side he did so with such force he partially went through it. He managed to drag himself out and make off again, but he had sprained his foot and took refuge against a chimney stack. After a short exchange Berry compelled Hindle to surrender, which he did before he was promptly marched off, along with Cockerel, to the police station, followed by hundreds of people who had gathered to watch the events unfold.

On Friday morning, Mr Mills identified the watches found at Hindle's lodgings as part of his missing property and the five prisoners – Hindle, Richmond, Elvin, Newson and Cockerel – were charged with robbery before the Great Yarmouth magistrates. Feeling no honour amongst thieves, Emma Richmond turned approver and gave evidence that on the night of the robbery Elvin, Newson and Hindle were together in her house, were out at the relevant time of the robbery, and that Hindle had returned with the gold and silver watches, which he then concealed in the chimney.

As if his escapades on the rooftop had not been enough for him, Hindle also attempted to escape from the Tolhouse Prison as he awaited trial, but he was soon detected and returned to his cell. Tried before the Great Yarmouth Quarter Sessions at the Tolhouse on Thursday, 9 October 1862 – before N. Palmer Esq., The Recorder – Henry Hindle, Elvin, and Newson were all found guilty of the crime and, as all of them had previous convictions proved against them, received three years penal servitude each. Cockerel, who was also charged with 'harbouring Hindle with a guilty knowledge', was acquitted.

Chapter Eleven

Witchcraft

A case brought before the Norfolk Assizes in March 1866 was widely reported under the headline of 'A Singular Case of Witchcraft'. The defendant was the landlord of the Railway Hotel at Wells, who had lost some spoons, while the plaintiff was a Mr Creak, who had been in his service. Creak's house and others had been searched to no avail but the landlord would not give up his search for the thief and sought the assistance of a lady in the district, who was known by the name of the 'Cunning Woman'. She had a reputation of being learned in the art of bibliomancy – described in court as 'a species of witch-craft.' Her method was to suspend a Bible from a piece of string and violently push it in one direction. Then, whilst it was spin-ning, the name of the suspected person was called out. If the Bible suddenly stopped spinning upon the utterance of the name, that person was the thief. When Creak's name was said it was claimed that the book stopped dead.

The landlord returned to the pub in a furious state and, having found Creak in the taproom with about five others, confronted him with the words, 'Bring them things back!' Creak replied, 'What things?' This was met with, 'Blast you – you know!' and, raising a poker, the landlord threatened, 'I could knock your head off.' His daughter then tried to intervene, but the landlord would

The quayside at Wells-next-the-Sea, *c.* 1900.

have his say: 'You are the thief, and no other man. I can prove it by the turn of the Bible. You have robbed the fatherless and the motherless. You got in at the window and no-one else.' The next morning, the landlord paid Creak his earnings to date and discharged him from his service. Creak brought a case of slander, assault and wrongful dismissal upon him as a result. The jury found in favour of Creak for the slander charge and awarded him £1 for damages, while for the charges of assault and wrongful dismissal they found in favour of the landlord.

The Walking Toad

A case was brought before East Dereham Petty Sessions in April 1879, in which William Bulwer of Etling Green was charged with assaulting eighteen-year-old Christiana Martins who lived near the toll-bar. She claimed that Bulwer had 'abused her' and in open court she repeated the obscene language and suggestions she claimed he had used – despite the attempts of the magistrate's clerk to stop her. The words escalated to an exchange of blows and as she attempted to fasten the gate, she claimed Bulwer hit her across the hand with a stick. Martins claimed she knew of no provocation for the abuse or the assault. Mrs Susan Gathercole was called as witness and corroborated Martins testimony, but added that Bulwer had claimed Martins' mother was a witch.

Bulwer blazed forth in righteous indignation and when Martins claimed she did not know the cause of the quarrel, he argued:

> Mrs Martins is an old witch, gentlemen, that's what she is and she charmed me and I got no sleep for her for three nights, and one night at half-past eleven o'clock, I got up because I could not sleep and went out and found a walking toad under a clod that had been dug up with a three-pronged fork. This is why I could not rest. She is a bad old woman; she put this toad there to charm me and her daughter is just as bad, gentlemen. She would bewitch anyone...She dug the hole and put it there to charm me, gentlemen, that is the truth. I got the toad out and put it in a cloth and took it upstairs and showed it to my mother and throwed [*sic*] it into the pit in the garden.

One of the sitting magistrates enquired if Bulwer went to church, to which he replied, with another excited ejaculation:

Bufo Bufo, the Common Toad, as featured in the Etling Green witchcraft case of 1879.

Sometimes I go to church and sometimes to chapel and sometimes I don't go nowhere. Her mother is bad enough to do
anything; and to go and put a walking-toad in the hole like
that, for a man who never did anything to her, she is not fit to
live, gentlemen, to go and do such a thing ... She looks at a lot
of people and I know she will do someone harm.

The Chair of the Bench had heard enough and asked Police
Superintendent Symons, 'Do you know this man? Is he sane?' The
police officer answered firmly, 'Yes, sir, perfectly.' The Chair of the
Bench said he was very sorry that Bulwer was foolish enough to
believe in such rubbish, and ordered he be fined 1s, along with
12s and 6d for costs.

previous to the tragedy. It was the habit of Charles Daines to start the fire and fill the kettle in the morning. When Mrs Daines took her tea and gave the children their breakfast of sop she used the hot water from the kettle. After just five minutes of drinking the tea she felt ill, her throat was burning, she vomited and soon the children were suffering the same thing. Fearful for their condition she had called her closest neighbour, Elizabeth Mills, who came to the house and had a cup of tea while she attended to Hannah and her family. Soon, poor Mrs Mills was suffering too and the whole sorry tale progressed from there.

The jury were convinced of Daines' guilt and returned a verdict of guilty after deliberating for an hour. After passing the death sentence, the judge implored Daines to repent and make his peace with God. Upon his return to his cell, Daines made a full confession to the prison chaplain and also admitted attempting the poisoning on two former occasions – once by adding arsenic to fried potatoes and once by adding a little to pea soup, both with little effect.

Charles Daines was executed on Saturday, 27 April 1839 on the scaffold erected just behind the gatehouses at the centre of the bridge over the castle ditches. He appeared to die an extremely hard death, suffering violent struggles and convulsive throes lasting for three minutes. One eyewitness noted that:

THE LIFE, TRIAL, CONFESSION, & EXECUTION OF

CHARLES

DAINES,
AGED FIFTY.

Who was Executed on Saturday, April 27th, 1839, for poisoning ELIZABETH DAINES, his Daughter, 3 years old, and ELIZABETH MILLS, his Neighbour, at HEMPNALL.

Illustration from the broadside sold at the execution of Charles Daines, the Hempnall Poisoner.

He clasped his hands, and raised his arms several times towards his breast as if in the act of prayer, unquestionably showing that consciousness had not left him. At length, his struggles became less severe and the awful stillness of death followed.

The body of Charles Daines was left to hang for an hour then taken down and carried into the castle. Sent for by his family the following Monday, he was buried in the churchyard of St Michael at Thorn, on Ber Street, Norwich.

The Poisoned Druggist

Albert Frederick Langford was a druggist on Norfolk Street, King's Lynn, and had enjoyed a happy married life with his pretty wife, Mary Anne, since their wedding in 1853. By April 1869, however, Albert's health had declined and he had been an invalid for about two years; he had become completely incapacitated and was unable to run his business – he was only thirty-nine. His wife, Mary Anne Langford (thirty-eight) had born him a number of children (seven of whom were living in 1869) with new addition, baby Charlotte, being born in January. The family had occupied a respectable position in Lynn, but Mary Anne was a troubled woman who had become gravely concerned for the future of her husband's business, due to his failing health. She feared that the family would be 'reduced to want'. She had become 'very low in spirits' and had even discharged their servants, applying herself to the household chores with only occasional help from a charwoman. Shortly before 8 a.m. on 27 April, Mary Anne sent for her mother-in-law, Mrs Susanna Langford. On her arrival Mrs Langford asked after her son, to which Mary replied, 'Oh, dear Mrs Langford, he is very ill, and the baby too.' Dr Lowe, the family doctor, was sent for and upon his arrival he discovered both Albert Langford and the baby suffering from 'strong tetanic convulsions'. Mrs Langford then said a very strange thing in a loud whisper, 'Doctor, I could bear it no longer: I have poisoned myself.'

'With strychnia?' asked the doctor.

'Yes,' replied Mrs Langford.

'And your husband?' he enquired.

'Yes,' she replied. At that moment Mary Anne was also seized by the same convulsions.

Another physician, Dr Archer, was sent for and these two medical gentlemen remained in attendance for the day. Mrs Langford's stomach was pumped successfully but it was too late for her husband and baby daughter, who continued to decline. Little Charlotte died at about 6 p.m., having suffered with convulsions almost continuously throughout the day.

A post-mortem examination was conducted by Dr Lowe and Dr Archer. Removing the stomach and stomach contents they placed them in a jar, fastened down by a bladder, and sealed it so that it could be sent, along with other viscera, to Dr Letheby for examination. A gown worn by Mary Anne on the morning of 27 April was also sent, after a small portion of strychnia crystals had been discovered in the pocket. A bottle containing about two ounces of pure strychnia, taken from a drawer in the shop, was also despatched in the hamper. It was noted that the drawer was not kept locked. Dr Letheby confirmed strychnia present in every instance, including the stomach contents.

Albert Langford also succumbed to the poison and he died on 6 May 1869. Mary Anne Langford, however, recovered and, after an investigation that extended over three weeks, she was committed to Wymondham Bridewell to await trial, charged with the murder of her child and a second indictment for the murder of her husband. One newspaper commented: 'A more terrible tragedy in English middle class life can scarcely be conceived.'

Mary Anne was tried before Mr Justice Byles at the Norfolk Assizes on Monday, 9 August 1869. The case hinged not only on the medical evidence but upon proving it was Mary Anne who had administered the poison. In an impassioned speech her defence counsel, Mr O'Malley QC, contended that there was no proof Mary Anne had administered the poison to her child wilfully or feloniously. He also argued that the comments she made to Dr Lowe and Dr Archer, to the effect that she had poisoned herself and her husband, were unreliable as she was not conscious of what she was saying at the time. He also mentioned that, due to her own poisoning, she was unable to reply properly to the questions that the doctors put forward. The jury were impressed with his argument and found Mary Anne 'not guilty' and she was granted liberty. No evidence was offered on the second indictment and, ultimately, the question remains – if Mary Anne didn't administer the strychnia to her husband and baby, then who did?

Vengeance of the Servant

Eighteen-year-old Charlotte Fisher was a servant girl employed by farmer Benjamin Barnard and his wife Sarah at Great Ellingham Hall. On 5 July 1871, a piece of linen belonging to Fisher hanging upon a hedge was damaged by one of the cows. Fisher was incensed and went to Mrs Barnard, demanding, 'Do you think I will put up with this? I will make Mr Barnard pay for his stock getting out – something I will do before I leave tonight.' Mrs Barnard took exception to this outburst and later that same day gave Fisher a month's notice, to which Fisher shrugged, 'If it is your wish, I will go; I don't think I have given you much trouble.' Later, Mr Barnard returned home for a tea that had been prepared by Fisher. Curiously, she had laid it all out in the dining room, which was dark and not the usual place where the family took that meal. Mr Barnard, tasting something disagreeable about the tea he had just sipped, refused to drink it. Mrs Barnard thought that it seemed to be 'blacker than it ought to be'. She poured more water out of the kettle into the teapot and noticed some bluish sediment in the water.

Suspicious of the strange substance, the contents of the teapot were sent to Mr Sutton – analytical chemist of Norwich – to be tested; a grain and a quarter of phosphor paste was found to have been mixed with the water. Just such a poison was kept in the house for killing mice and one of the farmhands claimed Fisher had come to him in a furious state of mind and swore that when she left she would, 'leave nothing alive on the farm.' Brought before Mr Justice Byles at the Norwich Assizes on Monday, 7 August 1871, Fisher was found guilty of attempted poisoning, but the jury recommended that mercy be shown on account of her age. Sentenced to penal servitude for life, the recommendation was forwarded to the Home Secretary, who reduced the term to ten years.

Chapter Thirteen

Attempted Murder

Thirty-nine-year-old Thomas Aldridge Sturley was not a man who was lucky in business. He had once kept a small farm but did not put much effort into running it and it eventually closed, so he became the keeper of the Bell Inn at Bawdeswell, which was declared insolvent in December 1843. Sturley needed work and so he became the driver of a coach that ran from Litcham to Norwich for a while, he then tried to find work in London but remained unemployed and returned to Norfolk, where he became a travelling agent for Mr Youngman, a wine and spirit merchant of Norwich.

Sturley was a married man with a large family to support. His uncle, Samuel Page, a wealthy Cawston farmer, had taken pity upon him and had even allowed one or two of Sturley's children to live with him on occasion. Page also lent Sturley money, but had tired of his nephew failing to pay it back. Matters became strained when Sturley, who had an interest in a property where Page was executor, asked his uncle to turn out the current tenants so that he might occupy it himself, but Page refused.

Sturley was a desperate man and his pleas to his uncle for assistance were made in such abusive and irritating language that it precluded any possibility of favourable attention being given to him and his family; indeed, it appears that Sturley became possessed with the firm belief that his uncle was bent on his complete and utter ruin.

On 19 November 1847, Sturley went to Page's farm at Cawston to tackle the matter man-to-man. Sturley met his uncle coming out of the farmyard, where he had been feeding fowls. Sturley hailed him: 'I am come to see you once more,' to which Page replied, 'So I see.' Sturley enquired, 'You have not done anything for me?' Page said, 'No, I shall not interfere until I have seen Mr Keith [his attorney in Norwich] I shall leave it all to him.' Sturley then accused Page, 'You have robbed me and my family of £600!' Page rebutted the accusation, saying he would make him prove his words and would not be scandalized in that way by him.

Sturley hesitated for a moment; he threw down his stick then put his hand into his breast pocket, saying, 'I have two little things here, one for you and one for me,' and promptly pulled out two small pocket pistols and cocked them both. Page noted they were both capped and ready to fire. Sturley then demanded, 'Damn you, are you prepared to pay me £250? You only have two minutes to live. Are you ready? Are you ready? – or off she goes!'

Page had half a peck measure in his hand and he waved it about his head to protect himself. Sturley then pulled the trigger on one of the pistols, saying, 'Off she goes!' It snapped but misfired, he then pulled the trigger on the second pistol; it did fire and the charge hit Page in the right side of his mouth, knocked out two or three of his teeth and caused him to reel back and fall to the ground. Sturley then picked up his stick and began to beat Page with it, saying, 'Damn you! Now you may hang me or do what you like with me!'

One of Page's employees, Samuel Douglas, saw Sturley fire the shot and came running. As he approached, Sturley presented his stick at him and warned, 'Damn you! Keep your distance!' After delivering one last blow to Page he walked away to the Rat Catcher's public house. Douglas got his master into the farmhouse before he went to inform the police constable of the incident and where he had last seen Sturley. Armed with this information PC Edward Ralph went to the Rat Catcher's and took Sturley, who still had the pistols on him, into custody. As Police Superintendent Edward Jones, from Aylsham, was conveying Sturley to Norwich Castle, he heard him say, 'What an infernal old rogue Page had been to my family. He robbed us of £600 and I could bear it no longer.'

Reepham surgeon Walter Harsant was called to attend to Page and extracted the shot from his face, and wadding in his tongue and mouth. He attended to Page for the next five weeks as he recovered from his injury.

Brought before the Honourable Sir Thomas Coltman at the Norfolk Lent Assizes in March 1848, after a trial that lasted little more than an hour, Sturley was found 'guilty of shooting with intent to murder' but with a recommendation to mercy. The judge then assumed the black cap, condemned Sturley for the heinousness of his crime, exhorted him to employ his time in making peace 'with his offended maker' and sentenced him to death. Most of those in the courtroom had clearly assumed a sentence of transportation or imprisonment was coming, not an execution, and considerable surprise and consternation was shown in court at this; not least by Sturley, who, aware that Page had recovered from his injury, had become convinced he would serve a term of no more than two years. He turned 'pale as ashes' and nearly collapsed in the dock. On Wednesday, 12 April 1848 a reprieve from execution was received by the governor of Norwich Castle Prison and Sturley's sentence was commuted to imprisonment. Sturley served his sentence at Millbank, Portland, Gosport and Dartmoor Convict Prisons before being sent to Gibraltar on a prison ship. He was finally pardoned, returned to the county and died in Bawdeswell in March 1883, aged seventy-five.

Broadside sold after the trial of Thomas Aldridge Sturley while he was still under sentence of death, March 1848.

The Lopham Slasher

Richard Roberts was a travelling draper and had been engaged to Eliza Hunt (aged twenty), who lived in a small cottage at North Lopham – but all was not well between the couple. Roberts was a jealous man and had become suspicious of the attentions a young man in the village was paying to Eliza. On Monday, 25 August 1862, Roberts came down to Lopham by the night mail coach from London. He went into the bedroom where Miss Hunt and her female companion, Miss Womack, were sleeping and, having announced his arrival, left the room to allow the women to dress in private. Miss Womack was first down; she then left the house, leaving Roberts and Eliza alone. Eliza set about preparing breakfast but was a little disturbed to see Roberts lock the door and pull down the window blind.

He then took her upon his knee and kissed her before he suddenly threw her down, knelt upon her and slashed her throat with his pocket knife. Although weltering in her own blood, Eliza called

A dramatic and imaginative artist's impression of the moment Richard Roberts attacked his fiancée, Eliza Hunt, at North Lopham on 25 August 1862.

out, 'Oh. Richard, set me on a chair, fetch me a glass of water and let me die in peace.' Her plan was to get her lover off her and if he did go for a glass of water she knew she would have a chance to escape.

There was only a chance that he would agree, but Roberts fell for her rouse and with her strength ebbing away Eliza managed to get away; she fell insensible into the arms of neighbour, Mrs Huggins, who had come running to help when she heard Eliza's screams.

The police were summoned and they discovered Roberts crouching under a bed in Eliza's room, lying in a pool of his own blood and a clasp knife firmly clenched in his hand. He had inflicted a fearful wound upon his own throat that ran from the back of his head and passing down to the front of his throat. The injuries he had inflicted upon Eliza were less severe and, fortunately, he had missed her carotid artery.

Eliza was carried to a bed in Mrs Huggins' house; at first it was feared she would succumb to the wounds she had received, but she slowly recovered over a number weeks. When Roberts was brought before Mr Justice Williams at the Norfolk Assizes in April 1863, he pleaded 'guilty' and, after making sure Roberts knew what he was pleading guilty to, the judge ordered Roberts to be removed so that he may look into the circumstances of the case. The following day, after commenting on the wickedness and selfishness of the act, and stating that his intended victim had recommended him to the mercy of the court, the judge sentenced Roberts to five years penal servitude.

The Foulsham Visitor

Forty-five-year-old Fuller Williamson, a hawker, had a vicious temper. His wife, having had enough of her husband's outbursts, became afraid to live with him and left the marital home, returning to live with her mother in a cottage near the Ship Inn at Foulsham. Williamson festered on the separation and after a long estrangement he arranged to see his wife at her mother's house, on the afternoon of 28 February 1878. When his wife refused to return home with him he drew a cut-throat razor on her and attempted to gash her throat. Mrs Williamson was, however, not

Foulsham Street in the early twentieth century.

to be trifled with and she resisted the attempt by holding the blade in her hand; in the struggle the knife fell and broke upon the floor. Williamson then seized his wife by the hair and began to beat her head upon the ground.

Williamson then grabbed the kitchen poker and with this formidable weapon rained down blow after blow upon his wife's head, demanding of her, 'Will you come with me?' She agreed, 'Oh, yes,' but the blows kept coming and Williamson replied, 'It's too late now, I may as well finish you off.' He hit her again and again until the poker struck against the floor and broke in two. He then attempted to drag her outside, where a policeman apprehended him and Williamson was charged with attempted murder. Mrs Williamson had been so badly beaten her skull was fractured and she was left insensible. She was not expected to recover from the injuries inflicted upon her, but recover she did.

Williamson was brought up on remand at the Reepham Police Court, bail was denied and he was sent to Norwich Castle to await his trial before the Norfolk Assizes. Williamson was tried on Saturday 3 August; he was found guilty of attempted murder and sentenced to twenty years penal servitude. Thunderstruck at his sentence, Williamson was removed from the court whining and howling.

Saved by the Hair

George Augustus Wilson was a hawker who, by 1880, had been living with Harriet Fox as husband and wife for eleven years at Highgate, near King's Lynn, and had one child together. They were not desperately well off, so they decided to take on a lodger named Henry Askew. Fox soon became enamoured with the lodger and the pair decided to elope to Oundle in Northamptonshire and start a new life together, taking the child with them – they even took some furniture with them. However, Wilson did not want to let Fox go and, embittered by the flit, Wilson used the fact that the pair had taken some of his property with them to declare it stolen and got the police involved. Fox swore the furniture was hers but the magistrates were not satisfied and sentenced the pair to fourteen days in Norwich Castle Prison.

On Saturday, 13 March 1880, Wilson went to King's Lynn Station to meet the train carrying Harriet Fox on her release from prison. While waiting there, Wilson encountered Fox's friend Elizabeth Bowen, who had arranged to meet Fox at the station, and engaged her in conversation. Wilson was clearly 'fired up' and told Bowen if Fox did not return to him 'there would be a murder committed before the night.' She thought Wilson was just making embittered threats and, although he was angry, was not unduly worried by him.

When Fox got off the train Wilson asked to be allowed to walk with her, she agreed and he endeavoured to persuade her to return to him. Unsurprisingly, after having served a short prison term because of Wilson, Fox did not want to know and just carried on walking with Bowen to a nearby pub, the Duke of Edinburgh, where Askew was waiting for her. Wilson followed her inside, where he tried once again to get her to return to him, but she refused to entertain him further. Wilson then spotted Askew and, in a fit of rage, went over to him and delivered a blow to his head with a stick before running out of the pub. With the fracas over they hoped that Wilson had gone away for good, but a short while later he returned.

Wilson had gone to John Youngs Potter's gun-maker shop on the high street and bought a pistol. This was quite a common event in

Potter's gun-makers on King's Lynn High Street, where George Wilson purchased his pistol, pictured shortly after it was taken over by Clough & Son in the late nineteenth century.

the late nineteenth century and would not have aroused too much suspicion (the requirement for a person to obtain a gun licence before they could buy a firearm with a barrel shorter than 9 inches was only introduced in 1903 under the Pistol's Act). Wilson, who appeared calm and reasonable, asked Potter to load it with a small shot and to be quick about it as he had a train to catch.

Fox and Bowen were still at the bar when Wilson walked back in and asked them to drink with him; they refused and turned away. Suddenly, Wilson presented the pistol and fired. In that instant Bowen pulled Fox's dress and the pair bobbed their heads. Wilson had fired his pistol in a crazed state; over thirty-five pieces of shot were found embedded in the wall, some had even hit their intended target – Fox. Wilson fled and local physician, Dr John Lowe, was called to the scene.

Fox had been wounded; the back of her head was swollen – two pieces of shot were embedded in the skin and another had penetrated the skull, but the majority of the shot to hit Fox was found to have been absorbed by the two pads of false hair she had been wearing! Wilson was arrested with some difficulty, for he was still in 'a wild state'. Brought before the King's Lynn Borough Magistrates, he was committed for trial at the Norfolk Assizes on a charge of attempted murder.

By the time Wilson was brought before the assizes on Friday, 23 April 1880, considerable sympathy was extended to Wilson, both before and during his trial. So much so that the judge, Baron Pollock, commented on it in his summing up: 'There seemed to have been a course of cold-blooded bad treatment to the prisoner by the man and woman.' In court, the question was also raised as to whether Wilson had acted with murderous intent or if he had fired the pistol simply to scare Fox and Askew. Wilson was found guilty of 'wounding with intent to inflict serious bodily harm', with a recommendation for mercy on account of the 'great provocation' he had received. A petition signed by many Lynn people calling for leniency towards Wilson was also handed to the judge before he passed sentence. Baron Pollock adjourned his decision to allow him time to follow the recommendation 'as far as the requirements of the law would allow.' After due consideration, Wilson was sentenced on the following day to eight years penal servitude.

The Wellington Square Stabbing

Make no mistake about it, the rose-tinted spectacles of nostalgia and the 'popular memory' of history often excludes the darkest aspects of Victorian life. The magistrates and assize court records of Norfolk, and indeed every county of Great Britain, reveal regular instances of violent behaviour, often fuelled by drink, in domestic situations. The following case was one of the more extreme.

Forty-three-year-old John Cullum was a coal porter who lived with his wife Eliza (aged forty-one), mother to their seven children, at Wellington Square, off Wellington Lane, Norwich. Things had not been well for some time between the couple and by March 1880, Cullum and his wife had been estranged for about three weeks. He had remained in the city and had returned to the house, usually in a drunken state, on a number of occasions and abused his wife. It was on 13 March 1880 when Cullum once

The vicious attack of John Cullum upon his wife Eliza at their home in Wellington Square, Norwich on 13 March 1880.

again returned to the house drunk, at around 9.30 p.m. When he entered he found a neighbour, Catherine Shaw, and his mother-in-law in the house; Cullum ordered and pushed them out of the room, saying, 'It is my house as yet.'

Cullum then began shouting and pushing Eliza about. Threats were pouring out of Cullum's mouth. He then put his hand into his pocket and Eliza was heard to cry out, 'I know you are going to cut my throat!' By this time Mrs Shaw had made it to the kitchen door and saw Cullum pressing his wife up against another door; as he stepped back Mrs Shaw saw blood pouring from a stab wound to Eliza's throat.

Mrs Shaw took hold of Cullum's shoulders and said, 'You will kill her!' As he turned she saw that he still held the knife in his hand and she turned to run into the kitchen. Eliza managed to get through the door and outside, but Cullum got hold of her and stabbed her again. In terror for her life, Eliza managed to wrestle the knife out of Cullum's grip and throw it away; however, she ended up on the ground with Cullum on top of her, about to start beating her with his fists. At that moment some men noticed what was happening and came running over. One of them kicked Cullum off, who then fled. Assistance was called and Eliza was removed to the Norfolk and Norwich Hospital.

House Surgeon, Mr Prior, would later testify to finding five knife wounds on Eliza's body; one of each side of the neck, a slight cut to the cheek, another upon the hand and the fifth just below the collarbone. She had lost a lot of blood and she remained in a dangerous state for days afterwards. The police were soon hard on the heels of Cullum and he was apprehended by City of Norwich Police Detective, Robert Rushmere. By that time Cullum had begun to sober up and claimed he was sorry for what he had done. Another detective, Robert Mason, found the knife, still wet with blood, in a nearby garden. Mason noted that beneath the blood it was quite clear the knife had recently been sharpened.

The case was brought before the Norfolk Assizes on Friday, 23 April 1880. Cullum spoke in his defence and claimed his wife had also treated him badly. Citing an incident, Cullum claimed that, whilst taking some furniture out of the house, Eliza attacked him with a chopper, a hammer and a piece of wood; all of which he had to remove from her in succession. He bemoaned the fact that she had brought him before the magistrates on a previous occasion, and considered himself vindicated because he had been discharged. He went on to claim that Eliza was 'also in the habit of getting drunk', that she was always swearing at him and the children, and that he had left because she had been away from their home all night on a number of occasions. He swore that she had also threatened to take his life on a number of occasions. After stating he could remember nothing of his knife attack upon his wife, but blaming provocation and drunkenness for his actions, Cullum at least admitted that he had 'lived a cruel life' with Eliza.

The jury retired for just a few minutes and found Cullum guilty of 'wounding with intent to murder.' In passing sentence, the judge commented that he thought it 'impossible that the jury could come to any other conclusion' and revealed that this was the sixth time Cullum had been brought before a court charged with making attacks upon his wife – the one previous to this being as recent as the February before. Cullum was sent down for twenty years penal servitude.

The Mariner's Lane Cut-Throat

Twenty-two-year-old Walter Martin was a carpenter by trade who had been working on Ber Street. He had been engaged to Miss Elizabeth Mary Ann Spurdens, an upholsterer, who lived with her family a short distance from his lodgings on Mariner's Lane, Norwich. Spurdens broke off the engagement of four years, against the will of Martin, in order to be with another man. On the evening of 18 July 1880, Martin saw Spurdens on Mariner's Lane whilst she was out on an errand for her sister. Martin asked Spurdens to go with him, but she refused; he caught hold of her and took her towards Bracondale. Spurdens remonstrated with Martin but he insisted she should accompany him to Martineau's Lane, where he sexually assaulted her. She ran away towards Bracondale and Martin called after her, but she kept running. He ran after her and, catching hold of Spurdens, pulled her into a gateway and requested that she kiss him. She refused. He then put his arm around her neck, pulled her head back and cut her throat with a knife. Martin then ran off and threw himself into the River Wensum at Old Lakenham, but failed to drown himself. He then went to Trowse and turned himself into the custody of the police.

Spurdens received rapid medical attention to her wound, and was remarkably fortunate that, despite the wound being quite deep and her life hanging in the balance for a few days, she managed to recover. Martin was brought before Mr Baron Pollock at the Norwich Assizes on Friday, 6 August 1880.

Giving evidence in court proved to be another ordeal for Elizabeth Spurdens, who had to be revived with milk as she recounted the horrific events of the night of her attack and nearly fainted at the close. Martin was found guilty of 'wounding with intent to do bodily harm' and sentenced to fifteen years penal servitude; he was sent to serve his time in Pentonville Prison, London.

Shooting at a Constable

On Sunday, 7 August 1887, at around 1.30 a.m., PC Davis was on duty on the road from New Buckenham to Kenninghall, when he heard a horse and cart coming towards Kenninghall. It was a bright moonlit night and PC Davis secreted himself in a hedge, in order to see what was coming. Shortly afterwards, he saw two horses and carts – the rear cart having a horse led by a halter trotting behind. PC Davis followed them into the market place, where he watched them go in the direction of Robert Youell's house. When PC Davis got in sight of the carts near Youell's house, they were stationary and a man remained in the rear cart who, upon seeing the constable, gave a low whistle, whipped his horse and drove off at a furious rate.

Davis approached the remaining cart and observed it was painted with the name 'A. Holl, New Buckenham' as he looked up from the side he saw another man (later identified as hard-ened horse thief and ex-prisoner John Raith) rushing towards him with a bludgeon in his hand, which was raised as if to strike. He demanded what the policeman was up to, to which Davis replied, 'I am doing my duty, what are you up to?' Raith spat back, 'What has this do you with you? These are my horses and cart and I am going to Suffolk with them.' Davis accused the man directly: 'You liar, that horse and cart belongs to Mr Holl of New Buckenham.' Raith went into the meadow and before PC Davis knew what was happening the other man was back, leading Mr Youell's horse away by the halter. Upon seeing the approach of the constable he shouted, 'Let the ★★★★★★ have it; shoot the ★★★★★★'.

PC Davis attempted to close with Raith, but he struck him across the temple with the bludgeon and was then struck across his face with a whip, Dazed, Davis followed Raith around to the back of the cart, where Raith drew a pistol from his breast pocket, pointed it at the constable's head and fired, saying, 'Take that you ★★★★★★, and if you want another you can have it.' Davis saw the bright barrel of the revolver in the moonlight and felt the bullet so close to his left ear as to numb the sense of feeling. Davis made a grab for the horse at the back of the cart and Raith retorted,

'You are at it again, you ✱✱✱✱✱✱!' and struck him twice on the helmet, breaking it, and once on his left hand, which had hold of the halter. ·

By this time Raith's accomplice had got on the cart, whipped it up and drove off in the direction of Garboldisham. Jonathan Cunningham, an off-duty police officer from the Metropolitan Police, and Mr Youell had come running when they heard the commotion but the cart and the assailants were gone by the time they arrived. PC Davis gave a full report to his Superintendent, and the descriptions of the men were sent to Scotland Yard. Raith had fled to London and was arrested there by Detective Sergeant White and Detective Constable Leech, who found Raith was still carrying the revolver. Raith was returned to Norfolk and identified by Davis whilst he was held in a cell at East Harling police station.

Brought before the Norfolk Assizes, John Raith faced charges of shooting at a police officer and for stealing horses, carts and tack from Arthur Holl at New Buckenham, and a bay mare and tack, the property of Robert Youells, at Kenninghall. Raith pleaded guilty to stealing horses but denied firing at PC Davis; his defence was based around questions of his identification and accusations of the witnesses telling lies against him. The judge and jury were unimpressed and when asked to consider their verdict almost immediately returned a verdict of 'guilty'.

When sentencing Raith, the judge listed a catalogue of his earlier misdemeanours dating back to 1873, when he was con- victed of horse stealing; he had received a month's hard labour and was sent to a reformatory; the following year he escaped and was caught horse stealing again and was sent down for seven years penal servitude, however, the same thing happened again in 1881. The judge had no hesitation in handing down twenty-two years penal servitude for his latest crimes. As Raith was taken down he said he hoped his Lordship might stay there until he came back. At the order of the judge, PC Davis was commended for his brav- ery and in recognition of his actions was granted a reward of £5 from the funds of the county.

A Mother's Love?

In December 1887, Esther Bacon (aged forty-one) had been deserted by her husband and was living in 'a wretched house not fit to put a horse in' on Row 37 in Great Yarmouth, with her three children: Bessie (fourteen), George (ten) and Ellen (six). Esther received no contributions to the support of the children from her estranged husband, so she found employment as a char-woman at the Yarmouth Workhouse, where she earned 7s 6d per week and was given her board.

While employed there she encountered a man named Tom Peters, who claimed he had £50 in the bank and persuaded Esther she should give up her job at the workhouse and go to live with him in Brighton. He came to Esther's house and stayed with her for a couple of days before he suddenly absconded. In the wake of this, Esther gave her daughter Bessie a penny and sent her on an errand to fetch half a pint of beer. Esther then instructed each of the children to drink some of it; they all did as their mother said, but Bessie complained it 'tasted like chalk'. Esther claimed that she had not put anything into the drink; however, Bessie noticed that her mother did not drink any herself, yet when she took the jug to the kitchen to wash it out, she put her fingers into the jug and put something in her mouth. Then they all sat down and, after a short while, the children began to vomit. Dr Lettis was called and upon his arrival he found all three children being sick. Although he saw no paper that might have contained poison, he did observe two white spots on the tablecloth, which he suspected might have been caused by 'white precipitate' – a poison composed largely of mercury.

Dr Lettis communicated his concerns with the police and Esther was taken into custody at Yarmouth police station. He saw her there and noted that 'she appeared excited but showed no signs of having taken poison.' When he suggested she had better go and look after the children, she replied, 'If I am allowed to go from here, I shall make away with myself by going over-board.'

The children were ill for a day or two but ultimately recovered; Esther's actions, however, landed her before the Magistrates' Court, where it was decided she would be sent for trial at the Norfolk

Assizes. Brought before Mr Justice Denman on Friday, 17 February 1888, Esther was found guilty on all three counts of 'administering poison with intent to murder' but with a strong recommendation for mercy. Before passing sentence, the judge left Esther under no allusions that she had been found guilty of 'nearly as high a class of crime as anybody could commit. If any of the children to whom you had administered white precipitate had died, you would have been tried and found guilty of murder.' He also sympathised that:

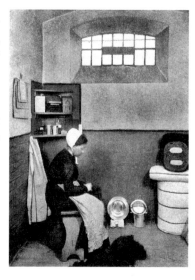

A female convict kept occupied picking oakum in her prison cell.

[…] in a certain sense she no doubt thought in her distress that what she was doing was not cruel. The children had not suffered, while she herself was a person of delicate health, which was likely to be impaired by sudden attacks. Thus it would be desirable that whilst she was undergoing imprisonment, she should be carefully watched that her bodily and mental health might be improved as far as possible.

Assured that arrangements had been made for the care of the children, Esther was sentenced to eighteen months hard labour. But, mindful of the jury's plea for mercy and her physical state, his Lordship added the codicil that when he said 'hard labour' it did not mean the treadmill of anything of that kind, but such labour as in the discretion of the authorities she was fit to endure. The point was, he felt, that she should be '[…] employed rather than kept idle in prison.'

Chapter Fourteen

Manslaughter

The Pump Street Slaying

Twenty-two-year-old James Flood was a hard man who lived in a hard part of Norwich. He had spent many years on Ber Street but had, of late, taken up with a young lady named Jane Field and they shared a dingy little upstairs room on Pump Street, near the castle. Both drank too much and when 'in drink' their relationship became one of abuse and violence. At 11.30 p.m. on Tuesday, 22 April 1851, neighbour Jane Smith heard Field return alone to her room drunk and soon heard her being sick. This sobered her up and as she passed Smith on the stairs she said she was going out again, 'after her sweetheart.'

Flood came back to the room, on his own, at 12.30 a.m. He was very drunk and made his way upstairs, but found he could not get in; he saw Jane Smith and asked if Field had gone to bed but she told him, 'No – she's gone looking for you.' Jane had gone off with the key, which caused Flood to fly into a rage, saying, 'Damn my bloody heart, I will find her and knock her eyes out and kick her bloody guts in.'

Broadside reporting the inquest and committal of James Flood to Norwich Castle Gaol to await trial at the assizes for the 'wilful murder' of Jane Smith in April 1851.

Flood came back down onto the street and went after Jane in a fury, and when he found her on London Street he violently set about her. Jane ran away crying out 'Murder!' but Flood overtook her back on Pump Street, knocked her down and kicked her mercilessly in the head as she lay on the floor. William Skelt, a nightwatchman, was on duty near the Crown Inn on Rose Lane and marked the time as 'about one o' clock' when he heard a female voice cry 'Murder' in Pump Street. He immediately went to the spot, where he saw the incident, and rushed to pull the male assailant off his victim. James Lefevre, another nightwatchman, also responded to the shout and Skelt advised him to take the man into custody while he tended to the woman. Skelt turned on his lamp and saw that Jane was covered in blood. He lifted her up and found she was motionless. Flood was still standing by and Skelt asked him if he knew what he had done, to which he replied, 'Blast her, I will kick her eyes out and so I will yours before I am done.' Both watchmen kept a firm hold on Flood – they managed to get the cuffs on him and he was taken to the station house.

Although hardly conscious, Jane was not dead and she was brought into Jane Smith's room, dripping with blood, her forehead cut an inch and a half deep, her lip was cut through and her nose broken. She vomited blood soon after. Surgeon William Day attended to Jane; hopes were raised for her recovery and even though he was by her side, there was nothing the good surgeon could do for poor Jane Field, who succumbed to her injuries at 7.10 p.m. on Thursday 24th.

The inquest was held on the Friday morning before Mr Mendham at the Eastern Counties Railway Tavern, St Peter par Mountergate. The jury returned a verdict of 'wilful murder' against Flood and a warrant was ordered for his committal. Brought before the city magistrates, the charge against Flood was reduced from murder to manslaughter and he was sent down for eighteen months.

Violent Drunkard

King's Lynn wood turner George Harold (aged thirty-two), was a selfish drunk who, despite being in full employment, used his money to finance his drinking habits, leaving his wife with insufficient money to put food on the table. Fuelled by alcohol, he would also subject his wife to ill-treatment. On 5 July 1878, Harold hit his pregnant wife's head with such force that it rendered her unconscious. Later that night the couple were in bed and Harold started teasing his wife. She told him to leave her alone and not to torment her, for it was his fault that she had an agonising headache. Mrs Harold's pains did not subside and she went to see Hannah Baldwin, a local midwife, confiding that she was 'dying from ill-treatment and starvation.'

Lynn surgeon Mr J.W. Barrett attended Mrs Harold and found her to be suffering from inflammation of the membranes of the brain, he also confirmed she appeared malnourished and emaciated. She died a few days later from exhaustion, complicated by her pregnancy. The post-mortem revealed that she had tubercular disease, degeneration of the heart and general emaciation. Brought before Baron Cleasby at the Norfolk Assizes, held at the Shirehall, Norwich, in August 1878, Harold claimed the blow that he had dealt upon his wife was, in fact, intended for one of their children and that he had hit her by accident. He also claimed he gave his wife fifteen shillings a week and paid the rent himself. Found guilty of manslaughter, when asked if he had anything

The Shirehall, Norwich, c. 1905.

to say, Harold replied, 'It was a bad day for me when I done it.' Harold was sentenced to five years penal servitude.

Trouble with the Neighbours

On Whit Monday, 29 May 1882, Mrs Eliza Newman went out, leaving her children playing out the back of her King's Lynn home in Whitening Yard. During the course of the day the children of the neighbouring Bailey family, who shared the same yard, asked to join in playing with the Newman children, but the Newmans did not want them to join them. In retaliation to the rejection the Baileys began to ill-treat the children and threw some water over them. When Mrs Newman's stepson, James Stannard (twenty-one), got home he went to protest about this incident to the Baileys and they set about him 'most unmercifully'; striking him upon the head and knocking him down. The women then took a brush and hammered him about the head until blood flowed from his nose and mouth. He did not appear to have struck a single blow himself. The following day, Stannard had been so badly beaten and his head was in such intense pain that he was unable to go to work. Despite receiving medical attention the pain continued, and on 9 June he was obliged to take to his bed; he went into rapid decline and he died on 16 June. The post-mortem examination revealed his brain was in a high state of inflammation that could have been caused by the blows he had received. As a result, William Bailey, Mary Ann Bailey, Elizabeth Maull and Harriet Ann Bailey were all indicted for the manslaughter of James Stannard, and brought before Mr Justice Hawkins at the Norfolk Assizes on Tuesday, 8 August 1882. The defence argued that the evidence was not sufficiently clear to convict the Baileys of manslaughter and tried to plea bargain 'for an assault which they did not for one moment attempt to justify.'

The jury returned a verdict of guilty against all four prisoners. In passing sentence, his Lordship said, 'the deceased's young life had been sacrificed to the brutal violence of the prisoners.' The court sentenced William Bailey to twelve calendar months of imprisonment with hard labour, while each of the women received eight months imprisonment with hard labour.

Justice for Lizzie Green?

Thirty-year-old Barnell Joplin, a corn meter from King's Lynn, and Frances Louisa 'Lizzie' Green (eighteen), a pupil teacher at St Nichols's Infant School, had been sweethearts for some time. They had been engaged for eighteen months, but the relationship seemed to have cooled after neither Lizzie's parents nor her headmistress at school approved of the match. By January 1889 Lizzie wanted to break it off. Joplin would entertain no thought of the matter and swore to a number of people, including his fiancée, if he could not have her then nobody else would.

On the night of 21 January the couple were walking along the staithe by the River Ouse, when they began arguing. Joplin pushed Lizzie into the freezing cold water. Filled with remorse, he then attempted suicide by throwing himself in too. The screams of Miss Green and the shouts of Joplin brought concerned people running and boats were put out into the high water. Joplin was wrested from the water in a semi-conscious state and was taken to the Crown and Mitre public house, about thirty yards away from where he was pulled out of the water. It was only some time later that he mentioned Lizzie.

A woman's muff was found floating on the surface of the river and, after searching for about two hours, her body was brought to the surface. Once the authorities were called, Joplin made confusing statements of how he and the girl ended up in the water, including: 'She pulled me in,' then in a later statement: 'I dived in after my girl,' and: 'She ran in and I ran after her'. On the morning after the incident, PC Edwards went to see Joplin and asked, 'Do you know how Lizzie Green is?' to which Joplin replied, 'All right for all I know,' then, after considering for a while, Joplin commented:

> She had a bad bilious attack last night, and we were on the quay for half an hour ... I had hold of her with my left hand and my stick in my right. When she went in I jumped in on top of her ... If she says I pushed her in I'll take the blame, I won't deny it.

The inquest jury were convinced it was a case for the assizes and Joplin was committed to trial, on the coroner's warrant of a charge

The River Ouse and quayside at King's Lynn during the nineteenth century.

of 'wilful murder'. At the Norfolk Assizes, Joplin appeared in the dock as a well-dressed man and at first did not seem affected by the proceedings when he answered to the charge firmly and clearly with 'not guilty.'

Surgeon Charles Jackson gave evidence that he had been called in to examine the body of Lizzie Green, but had not conducted a post-mortem so could not say what was the cause of death. Mr Justice Field expressed his opinion that as no post-mortem examination had been made, there was no legal evidence forthcoming as to the cause of death and he could not allow the trial to continue. The prosecuting counsel, Mr Mayd and Mr Justice Field, discussed the matter and Mayd said he would 'bow to his Lordship's ruling.'

Mr Beloe, the Coroner for Lynn, was standing in the body of the court and interrupted, 'I am the Coroner and I beg leave to say that every inquiry was made'. Justice Field demanded, 'Who is that man?' The Usher replied, 'The Coroner, my Lord.' The judge then replied, 'Then I pray that the Coroner will take himself from the Court.' Beloe acquiesced, 'I will my Lord,' but the judge went on, 'You are a professional man and ought to know better than to interrupt court in such a manner.' Beloe replied, 'I was only going to say...' but he was cut off again by the judge: 'You have no business to interfere here. I am surprised at you.' Mr Justice Field refused to hear anything more from the Coroner, the prosecution was withdrawn, and Joplin was acquitted and discharged a free man.

Mr Justice Field was known for his contempt of medical witnesses and was criticised in the *Journal of Mental Science*, April 1889, for his behaviour in another case, where, after 'treating the medical witness with studious rudeness, he refused to receive their opinion.' Mr Justice William Ventris Field retired from the Bench a year later.

Chapter Fifteen

Murder

Greenacre Pie

James Greenacre was born in the village of North Runcton, near King's Lynn, in 1785. His parents were farming folk and James exhibited considerable mental ability and promise in business from an early age. Aged ninteen, he commenced his own business on the London Road. That same year he married the daughter of Charles Wear, the keeper of the Crown and Anchor at Woolwich; this poor girl died suddenly. Greenacre married again – this time the daughter of a Romford landowner – but she too died, the cause of death being recorded as 'brain fever'. In those days of tragic mortality levels, death was a common fact of life; perhaps Greenacre was unfortunate, or perhaps he was a clever killer.

Fifteen months after the death of his second wife, Greenacre married a Miss Simmonds of Bermondsey. She bore him seven children but only two of them lived to maturity. It was around this time that Greenacre became associated with a group of radical extremists, who became notorious as the 'Cato Street Conspirators'. They hatched an outrageous, but ultimately abortive plan, to murder the entire British Cabinet. This association

James Greenacre

James Greenacre, the Norfolk-born man who became the infamous 'Edgware Road Murderer' in 1837.

got too hot for Greenacre – coupled with the collapse of his grocery business after he was exposed for fraudulent dealing – and he fled to America, leaving his wife and children behind. She died shortly after his departure; the cause of death was believed to be cholera.

Greenacre met his next prospective wife via a newspaper advertisement. Hannah Brown, a Norfolk girl by birth, was a tall and fine-looking widow, but she was known to have a bad temper. Hannah had been in the service of Lord Wodehouse at Kimberley Hall for about four years. Greenacre courted Brown, soon proposed marriage and they became lovers. Greenacre continued to live and conduct his business in London, visiting Hannah in Norfolk for their liaisons. He also maintained a number of mistresses, but became particularly smitten with a pretty, younger woman named Sarah Gale. Greenacre wanted to forsake all others and start a new life with Sarah. He was ready to break off his promise to marry Hannah when she informed him that she was pregnant and was going to come down to London, in full anticipation of Greenacre making good on his promise of marriage. Fearful that this would ruin his prospects with Miss Gale, Greenacre induced Hannah to come to his rooms, baggage and all, on 24 December 1836.

What he planned to do next is unclear; perhaps he was planning another 'sudden, but unfortunate death'; perhaps he tried to worm his way out of the situation and Hannah blew up into one of her fearful tempers. All that is known is that very shortly after her arrival, Greenacre struck Hannah one almighty blow over the head with a silk roller, killing her instantly. Greenacre then set about the grim task of disposing of the body. He decided not to try and move the whole unwieldy body at once – that would attract too much attention. Instead, Greenacre crudely dismembered her corpse using a knife and an ordinary carpenter's saw, then, under cover of darkness, dumped the body parts around London. The trunk of the body was found on Edgware Road, the legs on Coal Harbour Lane and, eventually, the head turned up after jamming a canal lock gate at Stepney!

When Hannah was missed by her brother, he found Greenacre and believed that his answers did not ring true. He took out a warrant against Greenacre and, when his apartments were searched, rags were found that corresponded with the rags that the body parts had been wrapped in. Greenacre stood trial; the evidence was damning and the jury only took fifteen minutes to return a verdict of 'guilty'. The case attracted massive national attention and a huge crowd bayed for his blood in front of Newgate Prison when Greenacre was hanged. Greenacre loftily sneered at the crowd and said to Calcraft, the executioner, 'Don't leave me long in this concourse.' The executioner completed his duty, and then, biting into a very fine pie, proclaimed the repast was so good, filled with generous chunks of meat, that it should be known hence forward as a 'Greenacre'; a morbid name which stuck for many years afterwards.

The Killing of the Fortune Teller

Denver, near Downham Market, has always been a quiet hamlet well off the beaten track and 'out in the wilds of Norfolk'. In the early nineteenth century this rural hamlet, like so many across the country, was occupied by country folk doing predominantly agrarian jobs, living simple country lives. In these times, before poor country folk could afford doctors, cunning men and women (often widows and widowers) would scrape a few pennies in their old age by supplying medicine, country cures, helping out at births, making love philtres and even fortune telling. For one reason or another, these marginal people had many myths grow up around them – one favourite was that although appearing poor, they were actually sitting on a fortune hidden somewhere in their house. One such woman was Hannah Mansfield, who lived on Denver Common. Even neighbours she knew well described her as a woman of 'eccentric habits', who was often seen about her house and the common late at night, or to lie-in beyond the usual hours of country people in the morning.

On the morning of Tuesday, 3 January 1837, neighbours thought nothing of not seeing her early in the morning, but when a woman brought a parcel to her door at 10.30 a.m. and received no answer, concerns were raised. When neighbours were told of the situation they went to investigate. The daughter of one of the neighbours noticed some blood on Hannah Mansfield's threshold. Struggling to open the door, the neighbours soon saw that Hannah's body was lying across the doorway, preventing the door from opening. Only by pushing her body out of the way could they fully open the door. Once it was opened they could see that the poor old woman had not simply collapsed, but were horrified to discover Hannah lying in a pool of blood, dead on the floor. Dressed in her nightgown, she had clearly come down to investigate some noise in her house and had fought fiercely with her killer, the final fatal blow being a violent and hideous gash across her throat. Upon closer examination, it was soon apparent that she had been dead for some hours.

A contemporary broadside depiction of the murder of the Denver fortune teller, 1837.

Once the Parish Constable and magistrate had been sent for, a search of Hannah's house commenced, revealing a sum of money thought to be in the region of £20 was. missing, along with a large amount of plates from her cupboard. Three strangers, all men who had described themselves as 'embankers', and later identified as John Smith (twenty-five), John Varnham (twenty-three) and George Timms (twenty-two) had been seen in the area before and after the crime. It was also known that they were on their way to Stamford via Doncaster.

Mr T.V. Wright, the Constable of King's Lynn, was sent aboard the Express Coach in hot pursuit of the suspects. With the assistance of the Chief Officer and Constable Wheater of the Doncaster Day Police, the rogues were tracked down to the notorious Bird-in-Hand public house at St Sepulchre Gate. Once discovered, it was noticeable that they were dressed in new clothes and had clearly been living high on the proceeds of their ill-gotten gains. Wright immediately placed them under arrest and brought them back to Norfolk in iron manacles. The three accused were committed to Swaffham Gaol to await trial at the next Norfolk Assizes. On 6 April 1837, they were brought before Justice Coltman and the trial commenced at 10.30 a.m. It concluded at fifteen minutes past midnight, when the jury returned a verdict of 'guilty', and the prisoners were sentenced to death. The sentence on Varnham was commuted after an ample confession by the other prisoners. On 29 April, large numbers arrived in Norwich to watch the execution of the two remaining – and by that time notorious – murderers on Castle Hill.

The Most Notorious Norfolk Murderer

The first crimes to really capture the public's imagination during Queen Victoria's reign were the murders committed by James Blomfield Rush at Stanfield Hall, near Wymondham in Norfolk, on 28 November 1848. The crime was the culmination of a tangled web of avarice and greed on both sides, which had many twists, turns and intricacies in a case that made very good copy for the newspapers. It held the public's imagination as each new revelation was revealed; books and broadsheets recounting every dramatic and lurid detail of the murder sold in unprecedented numbers. The broadsheet of the 'Sorrowful Lamentations' of the murderer sold an incredible two and a half million copies across the country. Rush's wax image, 'taken from life at Norwich', was undoubtedly the star attraction in Madame Tussaud's Chamber of Horrors in the last year of the great lady's life. Visitors were recorded as looking into his cold, glassy eyes with 'the most painful interest.' The notoriety of James Blomfield Rush ensured his figure was on display in the Chamber for over 120 years.

James Blomfield Rush, one of the most infamous murderers of the nineteenth century.

Rush was a farmer with pretensions of being a country squire, but he had a long record of dubious deals, and was always trying to find legal loopholes and wrangles to get himself out of debt or bad financial commitments. He also failed to defend suits brought against him for seduction and bastardy by more than one complainant.

By 1843, Rush was heavily indebted and his wife died after a 'lingering illness' at their farm in Felmingham. During her confinement to bed, it was noted that Rush was 'very attentive'. It is easy to be sceptical over his motives or possible interference which may have speeded his wife's demise, but her will did not leave anything to James; instead, all of her worldly goods went to trustees for the benefit of her children. Rush then forged a codicil that placed the property in his power until his youngest child reached the age of twenty-one.

On 3 October 1844 another family tragedy occurred. James's stepfather, John, was found dead in his kitchen from a shotgun wound. James had been over on a visit and they had been shooting together. James stated that his stepfather had been enamoured with his gun and he had left him to admire it in the kitchen while he

Potash Farm, the home of James Rush, 1848.

went upstairs to wash. James claimed he heard the gunshot, sped back into the kitchen and found, 'to his horror, the gun had gone off', lodging the entire contents of the blast in his stepfather's head – entering at the left cheek – killing him instantly. There were grave doubts that Mr Rush senior could have inflicted the fatal wound on himself but the inquest recorded a verdict of 'accidental death'. Mr Rush left behind an estate worth in excess of £7,000, but James Rush was not mentioned in his stepfather's will. However, he was soon able to 'borrow' a considerable sum from his widowed mother to help fend off his creditors and descent into bankruptcy. Rush's mother died in August 1848; later commentators would note 'her death being hastened by her son's misconduct.'

Rush was to meet his match in Isaac Jermy, the Recorder of Norwich, who knew the law and was not afraid to use it to his advantage. The mortgage from Isaac Jermy to Rush for his new home, Potash Farm, near Wymondham, was due for settlement on 30 November 1848. Rush had blown all his inheritance, he had no more sources of money to draw on and he was left with no way of paying it.

On the night of 28 November 1848, Rush walked the short distance from Potash Farm to Stanfield Hall, where he disguised

Stanfield Hall, 1848.

himself with a mask, wig and whiskers and hid in the shrubbery. When Isaac Jermy stepped out from the hall to take in the evening air after dinner, Rush shot him at almost point blank range. The masked assassin then strode into the hall, where he shot dead Jermy's son in the staircase hall, and wounding servant Eliza Chastney and Jermy's daughter as they fled upstairs.

Despite wearing a disguise, the bulk and gait of Rush were quite unmistakable and he was soon under arrest. Tried at the Norfolk Assizes in March 1849, Rush had arrogantly turned down offers of legal counsel and opted to defend himself; he was often belligerent and attempted to intimidate the prosecution witnesses.

Masses of column inches in local and national papers were devoted to the case, and large crowds packed the public gallery and gathered in front of the Shirehall to watch the comings and goings of those involved in the trial, in the hope of catching a glimpse of Rush. The drama was heightened still by the arrival of the injured housemaid, Eliza Chastney, who was there to give evidence. Her injuries were such that she was bedridden and still in considerable pain. A bed had been specially constructed to be carried by men in a manner similar to that of a sedan chair, except this had a tent-like canvas canopy and curtains. In this palanquin she was carried from

Stanfield Hall to Norwich in relays, which stopped at every forty yards. Escorted by County Police to Harford Bridges, the cortege was met by a large body of City Police under the direct command of Chief Constable Yarrington. The Norwich constables formed a line in front and a line behind, with the county constables at the side, thus this unique procession brought the star witness to the first day of the trial. From her canopied bed, this brave young lady repeated her account of the night and confidently identified the perpetrator as James Blomfield Rush. Despite the disguise she qualified her belief, stating that, 'Mr Rush has a way of carrying his head which can't be mistaken. No person ever came to Stanfield with such an appearance, beside himself.'

When Rush presented his defence he spoke for a marathon fourteen hours. His five witnesses were hardly worthwhile, even damning. Amongst them was Maria Blanchflower, a nurse at Stanfield Hall. She stated that she had seen the disguised murderer but did not recognise the figure as Rush, despite having run past within a few feet of him. Rush asked, 'Did you pass me quickly?' – an unfortunate slip of the tongue, especially in open court! After a deliberation of just ten minutes the jury returned a verdict of 'guilty' and Rush was sentenced to death.

April 21st 1849 was the date set for Rush's execution, and it drew a massive crowd. But Rush was not one to be denied one last snub, as one eyewitness recorded:

> The wretched creature looked for an instant on the vast mass of spectators, whose earnest gaze was upon him and on every movement he made, and then turned himself round and faced the castle – his back being towards the populace.

He shook hands with the governor, and then the executioner, William Calcraft, drew the white hood over Rush's head. Having already fastened the rope to the beam – he then set about adjusting the noose around Rush's neck. Unable to resist a last whinge a voice snapped at the executioner from under the hood, 'This does not go easy! Put the thing a little higher – take your time – don't be in a hurry!' These were to be Rush's last words. As the chaplain read the section requested by Rush, 'The Grace of our Lord Jesus

Christ…' the signal was given and the bolt was drawn, releasing the gallows trapdoor and James Blomfield Rush was no more.

After hanging for the usual hour, Rush's body was taken down and returned to the prison. In the afternoon, Rush's head was shaved and a cast was taken by Mr Bianchi of St George's Middle-Street, in Norwich. The remains were then buried within the precincts of the prison. No headstone was granted, as per regulations, only a stone tablet bearing the initials JBR and the year of his execution mark the final resting place of the man known to history and infamy as the Stanfield Hall murderer.

The Thurlton Hammer Murder

Thirty-three-year-old George Baldry had been known to the Warnes family for twenty years and had lodged with them for many years in their little house at Thurlton. Baldry earned his living working as a labourer on local farms or on the fishing boats out of Yarmouth or Lowestoft; he had never exhibited any signs of out of the ordinary behaviour, until 8 August 1850. Baldry would never discuss his actions from that day, so the account of the event comes from the dying declaration of his young victim, Caroline Warnes (thirteen), who dictated the following statement to James Copeman, Clerk to the Magistrates for the London and Clavering Division, in the presence of Mr Hudson, a magistrate:

When George Baldry came up to my bed he asked me when I was going to get up. I said 'Not yet'. I had then a cat in the bed. I was afraid he was about to get the cat and I covered it up. He then struck me a blow on the side of the head and another on the front. I put up my hand to save the blow and he struck my thumb. He struck me five or six blows on the head. After he struck me one blow I looked to see what he struck me with, but the blows came so quick I could not see. He sat on the bedside after he had finished striking me. I felt the blood run down my arm and then I got out of bed and he took me in his arms and downstairs into the kitchen and set me down on the bricks. I remained there about two minutes. I got up of my own accord and went into the wash-house and undone the door by drawing two pegs out. I went into the back yard and I called to my aunt, saying, 'Aunt, aunt! Oh come here!' She is Mrs Ives [she lived next door] I went back to the kitchen; George Baldry was there. My aunt came directly through the front door into the kitchen. Mr Minister came up directly after her. My aunt said to me, 'Who's done this?' And I said, 'George Baldry'. He was then standing by and said nothing. This question was put in the hearing of my aunt and Mr Minister. I first saw a hammer in Baldry's hand in the wash-house whilst he was hanging it up by a string on a nail over the saw. The same morning I saw the hammer covered with blood in the hands of a policeman. Before I went into the yard to call my aunt I saw Baldry hang up the hammer. My aunt took me in her arms into the cottage and Baldry followed us. My aunt told him not to go in and then he walked away. He said, 'Oh dear, what is the matter?' I have never quarrelled with him. I liked him very well. He sometimes run me about. My mother told me not to let him play with me. I once told my mother he did so. I do not know whether he knew that I told my mother. The back door and the front door were both fastened when I went downstairs. My father had gone to work and my mother had gone to Norwich. This statement is all true, and I make it with the feeling that I shall not recover.

This was signed with an 'x', the mark of Caroline Warnes.

Attended by surgeon Robert Pedrift, Caroline was removed to the Norfolk & Norwich Hospital where she had no less than six pieces of skull taken out of her wounds. She lingered between life and death for some days, but eventually died on 24 August.

Baldry had been apprehended on the road at Carlton near Lowestoft by PC Samuel Wright. Wright saw him sitting on the bank and stopped to ask the man his name. He hesitated and said 'Dunn'. He claimed that he came from Southwold and was on his way to Lowestoft. The man's demeanour did not satisfy PC Wright and he fitted the description of the wanted man, so he said, 'I am afraid I must take you up on a charge or murder.' The man replied, 'I can't help it now.' Upon this Wright asked if his name was Baldry and the man confessed, 'It is.'

Baldry was taken to Norwich Castle and was remanded before the magistrates. All Baldry would say of the killing was: 'I have nothing to say against my being remanded. I cannot say but what I have done it. I certainly did do it, but not for the purpose.'

Baldry was committed to trial upon the Coroner's warrant and appeared at the Norfolk Assizes on 28 March 1851. Witnesses gave their statements and Baldry's bloodstained waistcoat and the hammer – which still showed the stains of blood upon it and even a few hairs – were produced in court by Police Superintendent Hubbersty. Caroline Warnes' tragic statement was also read at trial. At first, when Baldry was called for by his own defence, he was unable to speak, but after a brief interval he said, 'My head is so bad I cannot recollect anything. I have only to say that I should ask the jury what reason they would say I should be supposed to have for doing this job?'

In summing up the judge, Mr Justice Erle, commented that 'the only question that might have reference to the degree of guilt was the state of the prisoner's intellect at the time when he perpetrated the deed.' His Lordship was of the opinion that:

> […] it was of the utmost importance that when a man had passed for a man of sound mind during the whole of his life, up to the time of committing a great crime, the doctrine should not be adopted that the commission of the crime was of itself, and alone, proof that the man who committed the crime was not responsible for the act.

The jury deliberated only a few minutes and returned a verdict of 'guilty'. His Lordship donned the black cap and the sentence of death was passed, which Baldry seemed to receive without appearing to be affected in any way. Baldry's sentence was later commuted to transportation for life.

The Elsing Murder

Agricultural labourer James Naylor lived with his wife Charlotte in a little row of cottages in the village of Elsing, near East Dereham.

They were an unusual couple as there was a thirty-year age gap between the two; Charlotte was an infirm old woman of eighty – who was partially blind, deaf and lame – while her husband, a man described as 'in the full vigour of life', was aged fifty-one.

During the evening of Sunday and the early hours of Monday morning of 20 and 21 September 1863, neighbours were disturbed by the shouts of James Naylor, who was making such exclamations as: 'Oh, my heavenly father, my blessed father,' and 'My blessed Jesus'. Naylor continued to conduct himself in an excited manner but on being remonstrated by Mr Matthews, a farmer of the parish, he desisted. Naylor remained quiet for the rest of Sunday, but when neighbours Charles and Eliza Isbell retired to bed they heard Mrs Naylor speaking to her husband, asking him if he was going to bed. Shortly afterwards, a light was seen in their bedroom and all seemed as if it would be quiet for the night. After an hour, Mr and Mrs Isbell were awoken again by strange noises coming from the Naylor's bedroom, when suddenly Mrs Naylor was heard to cry out, 'Oh, James, don't hurt me,' then a loud shriek, followed by a heavy rumbling noise, as if something was being dragged downstairs. There was another shriek followed by deadly silence. The Isbells listened intently, shocked and not really knowing what to do until the tread of heavy footsteps in the Naylor's downstairs room broke the silence. They could then discern the voice of James Naylor talking to himself and uttering wild proclamations through the night.

Neighbours, suspicious of what had happened during the night, forced entry into the house and were greeted by a horrific sight. At the foot of the stairs lay poor old Mrs Naylor in a blood-stained nightdress in a small pool of blood. Her body was partially doubled up and her head and arms 'bore the marks of the most cruel savagery'; one leg was clearly broken just above the ankle. A trail of blood was also visible where she had been dragged down the stairs. More extensive injuries were revealed after her body was removed for a post-mortem, carried out by Mattishall surgeon Mr G. Taylor. Mrs Naylor displayed severe bruising on the head and temple and a number of her ribs had been broken.

James Naylor was apprehended and when asked for his motive for committing this horrible deed, he stated that it was done in a

Norwich Castle Prison, 1862.

desire to 'obey his Heavenly Father'. Some believed he had acted under some form of religious monomania; others suggested the killing had been a result of an argument over some money that Mrs Naylor had put aside to pay the rent, which Mr Naylor had discovered and had other plans. Brought before a coroner's jury, Naylor was committed to Norwich Castle to await trial at the Norfolk Assizes on a charge of wilful murder.

While at the castle, Naylor's conduct caused concern that his mind was disordered, and his health declined. Mr Master, the surgeon, treated Naylor and he appeared to make some recovery before he suffered a sudden relapse and died on 23 November 1863. Despite efforts to secure a confession, the dying Naylor would only say he was sorry for what he had done. The post-mortem revealed that ulceration of the stomach caused by cancer had saved him from the noose.

Fury of the Fish Hawker

Thirty-six-year-old Arthur Riches was a fish hawker who had been married to his wife Matilda (thirty-one) for almost sixteen

Arthur Riches, the murderous fish hawker.

Mrs Matilda Riches.

years. Sadly, the later years of their married life had not been happy ones and Arthur had become a very jealous man. Arguments were frequent and he had even threatened Matilda with a knife, shouting, 'I will rip your bloody guts open!'

In late October 1886, Matilda could stand it no more. She walked out on him and took up lodgings with Mrs Amelia Howard on Colegate Street; but she was not alone, she was with a man and the couple represented themselves as a married couple – Mr and Mrs Larke. Riches resolved to get his wife back and set out from Beccles to do so on 8 November 1886. On his way out of the town he spoke to Charles Farman, a railway gatekeeper, stating: 'I am following my wife and if I find that she is living with any other man I will kill them both and then drown myself in the river!' Riches met his father on Gentleman's Walk in the city at about 8.15 p.m. and a little further along, opposite the Star Hotel near the Haymarket, they saw Matilda walking with Mrs Howard. Riches asked, 'What have you been doing here? To which Matilda simply replied, 'I shan't tell you.' Riches then demanded to know where she had obtained the brooch and earrings she was wearing. Mrs Howard

The murderous attack of Arthur Riches on his wife on The Haymarket,
Norwich, 8 November 1886, as depicted in the *Illustrated Police News*.

spoke up and explained that they were hers and that she had loaned
them to her friend. Riches replied by pulling one the earrings forci-
bly from Matilda's ear. The verbal exchanges continued, even Riches
father joined in: 'I know more than he does about this. I know what
she is doing here.'

Riches saw red and knocked his wife's head against a shop
door, demanding again, 'What are you doing here?' She gave
no response and he hit her against the door again, then Matilda
shouted, 'Oh Mrs Howard, he's got a knife.'

Riches got his arm around her throat and stabbed her in the
neck with his knife. Riches' father managed to pull him off and
Matilda went stumbling up the yard of the Star Hotel. Riches was
still possessed with blind fury and, shaking off his father, he strode
over to where Matilda was leaning against a wall and stabbed her
again. PC High was soon on the scene and asked the crowd that
had gathered, 'Who stabbed the woman?' Riches came forward
and confessed, 'I did,' then turned to his wife, who he had just
attacked and said, 'I will be hanged for you.' Just before he was
taken away, Riches reached down, took Matilda's hand and bid

her 'goodbye'. Matilda was put in a cab and rushed to hospital but it was too late; she was found to be dead on arrival.

At the police station, Riches said he would die for his wife and that he hoped she would die too. Tried before Mr Justice Field at the Norfolk Assizes on 23 November 1886, much was made of how Riches had been provoked to attack his wife by her actions, especially taking up with another man. The jury found Riches guilty of murder but gave a strong recommendation to mercy, on the ground that 'the prisoner had received great provocation'. Sentence of death was passed on Arthur Riches, but it was later commuted to penal servitude for life. Riches died at Parkhurst Prison on the Isle of Wight in April 1898.

Henry Stebbings – Homicidal Maniac

Henry Stebbings made the acquaintance of Miss Wiles, a young servant girl, while she was working at Attleborough. They had agreed to marry and the couple stayed with her family at West Bilney. What she did not know was that Stebbings had a criminal record; he had been sent down for nine calendar months for unlawful and malicious wounding in October 1868.

On Monday, 26 June 1871, Stebbings left the house with his fiancée's younger sister, Maria Wiles (ten), for the purpose of procuring work in the hay fields. The pair crossed into a field on the way to East Winch, where they both sat down on a bank not far from the woods. It was here that Stebbings sexually assaulted the young girl. He then put his arm around her neck, kissed her, told her he was sorry for her and proceeded to cut her throat before throwing her body into the woods. Passers-by heard the moans of the poor girl and, on investigation, found her and carried her to the Maid's Head Inn. The little girl was fortunate to have her wounds attended to quickly and was removed to Lynn Hospital under the care of Dr Lowe. Despite being in a critical state for some time, she did make a recovery.

Stebbings had fled and a search was carried out for him, led by Inspector Carter of the County Constabulary and Superintendent Ware. Stebbing's description was distinctive; he had a hump on his back, caused by a cart running him over when he was a young lad. He was soon traced, arrested and lodged at the county lock-up in Grimston.

When Stebbings was brought up on remand before the magistrates, young Maria was brought to the court from Lynn Hospital to give evidence. Her throat was still covered in bandages, and she was seen to shudder when brought before her assailant. The case against Stebbings was sent for trial at the Norfolk Assizes and upon removal from the court the crowd attempted to assault him. Stebbings was bundled into the police carriage and taken to the railway station, en route for Swaffham Prison, where he would remain until his trial.

Stebbings appeared at the Norfolk Assizes on Wednesday, 9 August 1871. He was found guilty of attempted murder and sentenced to ten years penal servitude.

Shortly after liberation from Dartmoor Convict Prison he was back in Norfolk. Reporting to the police station at Watton, he went to lodge at the nearby village of Saham Toney. On 21 October 1882, Stebbings was on the road at Saham when he encountered a young girl named Hannah Brett (eleven) as she was running an errand for her mother, taking her brother's dinner to the village school. A Mr Drew, who had been working at a nearby farm, noticed Stebbings behaving suspiciously by the side of the road and as their eyes met Stebbings ran away. Drew went to where Stebbings had been standing and was horrified to find Hannah Brett laying on her back with her clothes turned up and her throat cut. With her dying breath she confirmed it was the man Drew had seen standing over her who had attacked her. Stebbings was found about half an hour later, a short distance away, hiding in some bushes at the back of the rectory grounds; the bloody knife lay nearby. Brought before Mr Justice Grove at the Norfolk Assizes on 9 February 1882, Stebbings' defence attorney argued a plea of insanity. The jury remained unconvinced, found him guilty and the judge sentenced him to death. The date for his execution was set for Monday, 27 February 1882. Marwood, the executioner, had arrived in the city on Saturday and on that same day a respite was granted on the grounds that Stebbings had received a medical assessment, following an appeal to the Home Secretary, and had been found to be 'subject to homicidal mania.'

MARWOOD the HANGMAN

The executioner William Marwood, who had arrived in Norwich when the respite from execution was granted for Henry Stebbings on Saturday, 26 February 1882.

The Hypnotic Mr Clarke

Joe Clarke, born at Hilgay, was adopted by Mrs Clarke when he was just three weeks old and was raised at her home on Keppel Street in King's Lynn. Educated in the town at All Saint's School, he was always a personable lad but 'rather shy'. After leaving school he spent a short while working as an errand boy, but his spirit for adventure was such that he went to America in 1913 and caught up with his natural mother in Virginia. While in the States he furthered his education with a year at Princeton University, where he obtained some knowledge of psychology.

Upon his return to Lynn, Joe Clarke was a changed young man, with confidence and a worldly-wise demeanour far beyond his seventeen years. He confided in close friends that he intended never to have to work for a living because he had become a hypnotist. To tide himself over he rented a room on Lynn High Street and set up business as a wireless dealer in the daytime, while in his spare time he cultivated relationships with dozens of young ladies, all of whom apparently succumbed to his hypnotic influence. His powers of conversation were described as 'out of the ordinary'; he seemed to know instinctively what to discuss and what interested young ladies. If a relationship appeared feasible he would woo his prey with carefully phrased letters and beautifully composed poems, which clearly showed Clarke as 'a man of poetic fancy and literary ability'. But, the thing that drew the fascination of the ladies more than any other was his apparent 'gift of some mystic qualities'. All of them were quite unsuspecting that his diabolical plot was far from romantic. He used his 'powers' to get them into a situation whereby he could hypnotise them, not for sex, but so they would part happily and freely with their savings and keep him free from financial worries!

It later transpired that his major income stream did not come from Lynn girls but from two girls in particular – one in Southampton and the other in Halifax, Nova Scotia. Both women were blissfully unaware of each other, or the deceit of their Lothario lover. Having met, charmed and undoubtedly been mesmerised by Clarke, these women would write to him often, enquiring when they could meet him again. Clarke would then reply with heart-rending letters telling them that he was ill and unable to work and, as a result, he was unable to pay for medical attendance or the comforts he needed to aid his recovery. Both women responded generously to the imploring letters of their 'sick lover'.

Clarke quietly left Lynn and several broken hearts behind him in 1926, and began an odyssey of deception and hypnotism across the country. He was eventually caught out and was brought up on charges of deception at Shepherds Bush, before being sentenced to six months imprisonment.

In October 1928, Clarke, now living under the alias of Reginald Kennedy, was in Liverpool, where he encountered nineteen-year-old Mary Fountaine. 'Persuaded' to take lodgings with her and her mother on Northbrook Street, Clarke soon began to weave his way into Mary's affections (no doubt to avoid paying the rent).

Mary's mother, Alice, was less easily persuaded and she took him to task about his lack of a job. Perhaps he tried his best techniques on Mrs Fountaine, perhaps he was shocked at his inability to mesmerise her, we shall probably never know, but Clarke lost all control and strangled Mrs Fountaine to death. He then strode into Mary's room, announced what he had just done and declared that he was going to kill her too! As he attempted to throttle the girl, Mary managed to calm Clarke down enough for her to make her escape and to run out onto the street, raising the alarm.

Joseph Reginald Victor Clarke stood trial at Liverpool Assizes in February 1929. He pleaded guilty and freely confessed his crime. Asked by the judge, Mr Justice Finlay, if he realised the implications of his plea and confession, Clarke replied, 'Yes, my Lord'.

Including the sentencing of death, the trial lasted just five minutes. Clarke was executed at Liverpool Prison by Tom Pierrepoint on Tuesday, 12 March 1929.

Chapter Sixteen

A Tale of the Transports

This final chapter relates the story of Ann Webster, a nineteenth-century convict who had returned to the county having served a term of transportation to Australia. It appears, with only a few minor grammatical corrections, as it did on a broadside published by Walker of Orford Hill, Norwich:

Ann Webster was, at the age of fourteen, in Heckington workhouse – her parents having died some years before. From there she went to Mr Gibbs, shopkeeper at London. After living there [for] two years she left her place, in the company of a young man, who brought her to Norwich and, unfortunately for her, introduced her to bad company!

Having lost her character, the unhappy girl abandoned herself to a dissolute and profligate life and eventually took up her abode at the Holkham Arms on the Castle Ditches. After going through various scenes of debauchery and infamy, with a constitution broken by disease and a mind debased by moral guilt, she was induced to commit the crime of picking the pocket of a gentleman who was in a state of intoxication; robbing him of his pocketbook and three £5 notes. Tried at the assizes she was found guilty and was sentenced to fourteen years transportation.

In her passage from Britain to New South Wales she described the hardships she endured on board the convict ship as 'beyond the imagination to conceive'. Two hundred and twenty male and female convicts were stowed together in a space so small that they scarcely had room to breathe. And, with most of them being of the lowest description of thieves and prostitutes, there were horrid scenes of blasphemy and guilt! And such reckless indifference to their fate shown by these unhappy wretches was enough to make the blood run cold to witness. This unhappy girl, used as she was to a dissolute and abandoned life for the last two years, still shuddered with horror at the wretched scenes of depravity she witnessed in that ship.

On her arrival at New South Wales she, with thirty other women, was immediately sent to Sydney and employed in the very lowest drudgery and laborious employment. They were not like the male convicts – condemned to work in chain gangs – who were employed in work that was only to be endured by men. They scarcely had clothing sufficient to cover them and were lodged all together at night in a single, miserable hovel with a little straw littered down to serve them for bedding. Early in the morning they were roused by their Task Master from their wretched pallet and driven without mercy to their work in the fields, or woods as occasion might be. Here they toiled twelve hours a day with just sufficient food to keep body and soul together, still it was a common occurrence to see one or other of these unfortunate wretches drop dead from fatigue and exhaustion; the body was removed and interred with as little ceremony as that of a dog would have been.

After two years in this scene of suffering, her health and strength sunk under the hardships she endured and her frame became so emaciated that in spite of the whip and the cruel overseer, she was, one morning, totally unable to crawl to her employment. As a consequence she was left behind, but her illness was increasing and she was removed to hospital. Under the direction of Mr Joseph Sylvester, the surgeon, she received kind treatment and shortly recovered, and afterwards had the good fortune to be taken as a household servant in the family of an English gentleman residing in Sydney. Having conducted herself to the satisfaction of the family, the stigma of her being a convict was forgotten and she was treated in all respects with kindness and consideration. She continued with this family for six years, during which time she had frequent occasion to attend the market at Sydney, where she was surprised to see many of the dissolute companions of her former life before she left Norwich – some in the most wretched and depraved conditions. And what is more remarkable, others whom she had known as the most abandoned characters in Norwich had, by a perfect reformation and sincere repentance, became not only useful members of society, but were also in a prosperous situation of life. One man in particular by the name of Randall, a most dissolute character in Norwich, was now in good circumstances in the hardware line, had a good shop and hands employed. A woman, by the name of Mary White in Norwich, commonly called Poll White, after enduring numberless hardships for years, is now situated in a decent public house in Sydney and is supposed to have accumulated considerable property. A man by the name of Onion who was transported from Norwich sixteen or eighteen years ago, is now in a very extensive business as a nail and horseshoe maker and employs a great number of hands and has, in fact, paid the passage of some of his relations from Norwich – having a good prospect of employing them in that line – to the colony.

On the other hand, Ann Webster declared she saw several emaciated objects crawling about the streets of Sydney, in the most destitute state of starvation, their sentence of transportation served but having no means to return to England, their conduct having been so bad in the colony that no person will employ them. One man in particular, by the name of Iky Harking, whom Webster had known as one of her dissolute companions on the Castle Ditches; this man, for his moral depravity and wicked conduct, had been frequently severely punished in the colony and was now in appearance an aged and emaciated object, although scarcely in his prime. The narrator declares it made her chill with horror to hear what he had been through, which he acknowledged was owing in a great measure to his own wicked and incorrigible inclinations.

He informed her that several of his companions who were transported with him have since been hanged for robbery and murder and that one in particular, who formerly sold oysters in Norwich, was not long since executed for stabbing his master through the heart whilst at work with him in the garden.

From this horrid tale of depravity of her countrymen the narrator returned home – reflecting upon the misery and wickedness that their sins brought upon themselves, to the prosperity and happiness that even a suffering convict may obtain by a sincere reformation of conduct, and a determined resolution to amend their future lives. After living two years more with credit in the family she was placed with, she found a strong inclination to re-visit her native land, for, although her parents were dead, she had brothers and sisters living whom she had a great desire to see. Accordingly, through the influence of her master and from her own good conduct, a free passage was granted to her in one of His Majesty's Packets bound for England, where she arrived, and landed at Liverpool the latter end of February and immediately proceeded back to Norfolk and was received by her surviving relatives as one that had risen from the grave!

After a little time she thought it might not be uninteresting to publish a short account of her adventure and that it might possibly prove useful in deferring others from giving way to idle and dissolute habits, which certainly leads to shame, disgrace and suffering.

Select Bibliography

BOOKS

Atholl, Justin, *Shadow of the Gallows*, (London, 1954)

Ibid., *The Reluctant Hangman*, (London, 1956)

Beecheno, F.R., *Notes on Norwich Castle* (revised edition) (Norwich, 1896)

Berry, James, *My Experiences as an Executioner*, (London, 1892)

Brend, William A., *A Handbook of Medical Jurisprudence and Toxicology*, (London, 1919)

Butcher, Brian David, *'A Movable Rambling Police' An Official History of Policing in Norfolk*, (Norwich, 1989)

Chapman, Pauline, *Madame Tussaud's Chamber of Horrors*, (London, 1984)

Church, Robert, *Murder in East Anglia* (new edition), (London, 1993)

Ibid., *More Murder in East Anglia*, (London, 1990)

Daynes, J. *The History of Norwich*, (Norwich, 1848)

Eddleston, John J., *The Encyclopaedia of Executions*, (London, 2002)

Evans, Stewart P., *Executioner: The Chronicles of James Berry Victorian Hangman*, (The History Press, Stroud, 2004)

Hillen, Henry J., *History of the Borough of King's Lynn*, 2 Vols (Norwich, 1907)

Hipper, Kenneth, *Smuggler's All*, (Norfolk, 2001)

Holmes, Neil, *The Lawless Coast*, (Norfolk, 2011)

Jarvis, Stan, *Smuggling in East Anglia*, (Newbury, Berkshire, 1987)

Lambton, Arthur, *Echoes of Causes Celebres*, (London, 1931)

Leigh Hunt, A., *The Capital of the Ancient Kingdom of East Anglia*, (London, 1870)

Mackie, Charles, *Norfolk Annals*, 2 Vols (Norwich, Norfolk Chronicle, 1901)

Morson, Maurice, *Norwich Murders*, (Barnsley, 2006)

Ibid., *Norfolk Mayhem and Murder*, (Barnsley, 2008)

Muskett, Paul, *'Riotous Assemblies' Popular Disturbances in East Anglia 1740-1822*, (Ely, 1984)

Palmer, Charles John, *The Perlustration of Great Yarmouth, with Gorleston and Southtown*, 3 Vols (Great Yarmouth, Norfolk, 1872–4–5)

Richings, Derek and Roger Rudderham, *Strange Tales of East Anglia*, (Seaford, East Sussex: S.B. Publications, 1998)

Rolfe, Fred and Rider Haggard, L. (ed.), *I Walked by Night*, (London, 1935)

Teignmouth Shore, W. (ed.) *Crime and Its Detection*, (London. 1932)

Ibid., (ed.) *Trial of James Blomfield Rush*, (Glasgow. 1928)

Sotherton, Nicholas, *The Commoyson in Norfolk*, (*c.* 1549) republished and edited by Susan Yaxley, (Guist, Norfolk, 1987)

Storey, Neil R., *Hanged at Norwich*, (The History Press, Stroud, 2011)

Ibid., *Norfolk Murders*, (The History Press, Stroud, 2006)

Ibid., *Norfolk Tales of Mystery and Murder*, (Newbury, Berkshire, 2009)

Ibid., *The Victorian Criminal*, (Shire, 2011)

White, Francis, *History, Gazetteer and Directory of Norfolk*, (Sheffield, 1854)

White, William, *History, Gazetteer and Directory of Norfolk*, (Sheffield, 1890)

NEWSPAPERS AND JOURNALS

Bury and Norwich Post

Dereham and Fakenham Times

East Anglian Magazine

East Anglian Notes and Queries

Eastern Counties Collectanea

Eastern Daily Press

Eastern Evening News

Family Tree Magazine

Famous Crimes

Norfolk Chronicle

Norfolk Fair

Norfolk Journal & East Anglian Life

Norwich Gazette

Norwich Mercury

Illustrated London News

Illustrated Police News

Penny Illustrated Paper

Police Gazette

Reynolds News

The Standard

The Times

Yarmouth Mercury